KU-575-578

Daniel Allen and Sons,

CABINET MAKERS, UPHOLSTERERS, UNDERTAKERS.
FURNITURE REMOVERS, VALUERS,
CARPET FACTORS, BEDDING MANUFACTURERS,

STATION ROAD, AND OXFORD COLWYN BAY.
BUILDINGS, CONWAY ROAD,

Brinsmead, Allison, Squires, Brockwood, and other makes of Pianos for Sale or Hire.

Estimates given for all kinds of Furnishings, Removals and Storage.

Glass and China Department.

Dinner, Tea, Dessert, and Toilet Services.
EVERY DESCRIPTION OF ENGLISH AND FOREIGN
GLASS AND CHINA.

Being Manufacturers of every kind of Furniture, Bedding, &c., we can guarantee
the quality of every article.

Colwyn Bay Hotel,

Chester and Holyhead Railway, North Wales Coast.

This Hotel is delightfully situated on the borders of the Bay, within a few minutes' walk of Colwyn Bay Railway Station. It is fitted up with every comfort and convenience.

The Coffee Room and Ladies' awing oom

Are on the Ground Floor, overlooking the Bay and Terraces.

THE BILLIARD AND SMOKE ROOM

Is also on the Ground Floor.

The Sanitary arrangements throughout the Hotel are on the latest improved system.

EXCELLENT BATHING   SEA WATER BATHS IN THE HOTEL.

Colwyn Bay is strongly recommended by eminent Medical Men for the mildness and dryness of its Climate.

COACHES to Bettws-y-coed, Llandudno, Great Ormeshead, viewing Conway Castle, Abergele, Marble Church and St. Asaph, starting from and returning to the Hotel.

Hotel Porters, in SCARLET uniform, attend all Trains, and remove LUGGAGE to and from the Hotel. STABLES, with loose boxes, and lock-up Coach House in connection with the Hotel.

MISS JONES,
MANAGER.

National Telephone No. 9, Colwyn Bay.

MOON'S

Commercial & Temperance

HOTEL AND RESTAURANT,

STATION ROAD,

 ## COLWYN BAY.

The new Dining Saloon now open for the accommodation
of 200 persons.

SCHOOL AND PICNIC PARTIES
SPECIALLY CATERED FOR.

HIGH-CLASS CONFECTIONERY.

CAMBRIDGE SAUSAGES AND MEAT PIES
FRESH DAILY.

HOVIS BREAD AND BISCUITS.
POTTED MEATS.

❀ SUMNER, ❀

Pastry Cook and Confectioner,

LLANDUDNO & COLWYN BAY.

.. Ball Parties and Wedding Breakfasts ..

SPECIALLY CATERED FOR.

ENGLISH AND FOREIGN

CHOCOLATES AND SWEETS.

ICES.

LONDON HOUSE, ⊚

~⊚⊚~ COLWYN BAY.

J. O. JONES' ..

Emporium of Fashion.

CELEBRATED ESTABLISHMENT

for MILLINERY, Welsh Manufactured Goods of all kinds. Choice Dress Materials. Fashionable Costumes, Mantles, Coats, Furs, &c. Household Linens in great variety.

MOST CHOICE STOCK OF FANCY GOODS.
DRESSMAKING UNDER EFFICIENT MANAGEMENT.

IMPERIAL HOTEL,

COLWYN BAY.

Beautifully situated near the Sea and New Promenade.

First=Class Accommodation for Families & Tourists.

BOARDING TERMS.—Children under 10 years of age, Half-price.

TABLE D'HOTE.

 SEPARATE TABLE.

Address THE MANAGERESS.

JOSEPH ARUNDALE,
Fruiterer, Fish and Game Dealer,

4, QUEEN'S BUILDINGS,
STATION ROAD,

National Telephone, No. 16. ## COLWYN BAY.

J. BARKER,
LADIES & GENTLEMEN'S HAIRDRESSER,
STATION ROAD, COLWYN BAY.

Prize Winner in Artistic Coiffure at the British Hairdresser's Academy.

Hairwork of all descriptions done on the Premises.

Ladies' and Gentlemen's Shampooing, &c., with all the latest and best appliances.

ROYAL HOTEL,

✸   ✸   COLWYN BAY.

. . Wines and Spirits. . .

WORTHINGTON'S ALES AND GUINNESS' STOUT.

FAMILIES SUPPLIED.

CIGARS OF THE CHOICEST BRANDS.

GOOD STABLING.   T. BYRNE,

PROPRIETOR.

Central Hotel, Colwyn Bay

WINES

Direct from the Vineyard. Pure Dinner CLARET, ONE SHILLING per bottle.
Prime Old PORT and SHERRY. BURGUNDIES specially consigned from the
famous Cote d'Or District. MOSELLE, HOCK, and CHAMPAGNE of the
best brands.

AUSTRALIAN WINES.

WINCARNIS.   HALL'S COCA WINE.   MINERAL WATERS.

OLD SCOTCH and IRISH WHISKEY, Specially Bonded.
All the best brands supplied.

COGNAC BRANDY, MARTELL'S, HENESSEY'S ; Superb 20 year old, 5/- per bottle
FOREIGN SPIRITS and LIQUEURS. LONDON and HOLLANDS GIN. JAMAICA
RUM. Special CORNER WHISKEY.

ALE AND PORTER BOTTLER.

BASS'S ALE, GUINNESS'S STOUT, 2/3 per dozen Half-pint Bottles.
**SOAMES'S PRIZE MEDAL WELSH PALE ALE and DOUBLE
STOUT,** 2/- per dozen. Both productions have high Medical Recommenda-
tion, and are guaranteed genuine ; tonic and digestive ; brewed from the finest
Malt and Hops with the Purest Water in Wales.

FAMILIES SUPPLIED.   ORDER OFFICE : **CONWAY ROAD.**

A. Robinson, Wine and Spirit Merchant, Colwyn Bay.

MARINE HOTEL,

COLWYN, NORTH WALES.

THIS Hotel stands in a beautiful position, overlooking the Sea and a broad expanse of delightful scenery, about five minutes walk from Station and Promenade. On the High Road leading from Rhyl and Chester.

The Hotel contains elegant Hall and spacious Dining Room.

LADIES' DRAWING ROOM.   ∴

PRIVATE SITTING ROOMS.

SMOKE ROOMS AND ·BILLIARD ROOM.

Colwyn is strongly recommended by eminent medical men for its mildness and dryness of its climate, and being warm and sheltered in winter is a most desirable resort for invalids.

POSTING IN ALL ITS BRANCHES.

J. W. LLOYD, PROPRIETOR.

TELEPHONE
No. 1.

TELEGRAMS:
"MEWS,
COLWYN BAY."

EDWIN JONES' COACHES.

TIME OF STARTING & RETURNING.

THE LOOP.—DUKE OF YORK leaves the Mews 9.45 a.m.;
Returning, 6.45 p.m.
Fare, 10/- ; Box Seats, 2/- extra. 56 miles.

TO AND FROM BETTWS-Y-COED.—A FOUR-IN-HAND
COACH leaves the Mews daily at 10 a.m. (weather and other
circumstances permitting, Sundays excepted) ; Returning at
6.30 p.m.
Fare for the Round, 7/- ; Box Seats, 1/- extra. 40 miles.

TO AND FROM PENMAENMAWR.—THE TOURIST
leaves the Mews 2.30 p.m. ; Returning, 6.15 p.m.
Fare, 4/- ; Box Seats, 1/- extra. 23 miles Round.

**TO & FROM RHUDDLAN CASTLE, CITY of St. ASAPH,
MARBLE CHURCH, & KINMEL DEER PARK.**
YE OLDE TIMES leaves the Mews, 11 o'clock ; Returning, 5.15.
Fare, 5/- ; Box Seats, 1/- extra. 28 miles Round

TO AND FROM BODNANT HALL, on Tuesdays and
Saturdays only. Leaves the Mews, 2.30 p.m ; Returning 6.0 p.m.
Fare 3/- ; Box Seats, 1/- extra. 16 miles.

ANY OF THE COACHES CAN BE ENGAGED PRIVATELY AT A
DAY'S NOTICE.

TANDEM DOG CARTS, 3/- per hour. PONY TRAP from 2/-
per hour.

BOOKING AND INQUIRY OFFICE:—THE MEWS, COLWYN BAY.

Carriages of all description for Hire ; Pairs and Single. For further particulars,
see EDWIN JONES' COACHING GUIDE.

*The only Carriage Proprietor in Colwyn Bay who has permission to
drive through the Grounds of GWRYCH CASTLE, the residence
of the Earl of Dundonald, any day except Sunday.*

(left margin, rotated) ☞ Should weather or other circumstances prevent the Coach from going, the Fare will be returned.

(right margin, rotated) In case of wet weather, each Coach is provided with Waterproof Aprons and Capes.

LLANDRILLO – YN – RHOS

A complilation of
'An Archaeological History of Llandrillo-Yn-Rhos'
by Rev. W. Venables-Williams
and
'Llandrillo-Yn-Rhos. A Souvenir'
by Rev. T. E. Timothy

Cyngor Sir **CLWYD** County Council
Library & Information Service
This book is number

283

of a limited edition of 375 copies

This compilation specially produced
by
Cedric Chivers Ltd, Bristol
for the publishers
The Library & Information Service
Cyngor Sir **Clwyd** County Council
Mold, Clwyd
1993

ISBN 0 900121 54 8

Printed in Great Britain by
Cromwell Press Ltd, Broughton Gifford, Wilts.
Bound by Cedric Chivers Ltd, Bristol

REV. W. VENABLES-WILLIAMS, M.A.

AN

Archaeological History .

OF

. . Llandrillo=yn=Rhos

AND THE IMMEDIATE
NEIGHBOURHOOD, . .

BY THE

Rev. W. Venables=Williams,

M.A. OXON.,

VICAR OF LLANDRILLO-YN-RHOS.

COLWYN BAY

R. E. JONES & BROS., PRINTERS, "WEEKLY NEWS" OFFICE.

Preface. . .

THIS little Hand-book is not intended to be a Guide to the Parish of Llandrillo-yn-Rhos, but rather a kind of Archæological history of the Parish and the surrounding district.

The object is to instruct and amuse, with no pretentions to originality, as it really and honestly is a compilation from various sources of interesting facts, which in all probability are known only to the few.

I cordially thank Archdeacon Thomas, M.A., author of a History of the Diocese of St. Asaph, and also the Rev. Elias Owen, F.S.A., Vicar of Llanyblodwel, for their kind permission to make any extracts I pleased from their valuable works.

I am under special obligation to the Rev. Meredith Hughes, F.R. Hist. S., St. Catherine's, Colwyn, for placing at my entire disposal his as yet unpublished notes on the submergence of Morfa Rhiannedd, and also on other most interesting facts connected with this ancient Parish.

Llandrillo=yn=Rhos. . .

THE Parish of Llandrillo-yn-Rhos (Llandrillo on the common, marsh, or plain)—is partly in the County of Denbigh, partly in that of Carnarvon. Rhôs, in some old documents called "Roos" and "Ross," signifies table-land, an elevated tract, a mountain plain, a flat or gently undulated region, elevated above a neighbouring level, whether the latter be land or sea. The ancient Cantref or Hundred* of Rhôs comprehended that promontory† which lies between the estuary of the Conway and the Bay of Abergele.

"Llan" is by some supposed to be the same as Saint; I do not think it is so: the word "Llan" is the Celtic form of the Latin "Planum" and originally meant "cultivated ground." In course of time, when all the cultivated ground had been fenced in, the idea of cultivation was gradually lost in that of enclosure and "Llan" came to mean "an enclosure" whether cultivated or uncultivated, such as Ydlan—an enclosure for corn; Gwinllan—for vines; Corlan (old Gaelic or Celtic for shed—sheepfolds). Finally the word acquired a restricted application to "THE Enclosure," "THE God's Acre"—"The Churchyard of the Parish."

The Rev. John Walters, in his well-known English-Welsh Dictionary, gives "In Church and State—mewn Llan a Llys" "Church-lands—tir-llan."

"Llan" also answers very much to the Greek word TEMEVOS—a portion of land set apart for a particular person or god, sacred enclosure—sanctuary, and for this reason it has become associated with 'Saint.'

From enquiries I have carefully made I find that the Parish was known in the 6th Century as "Dinerth Goch Rufonioc."‡ "In A.D.

---

*Cantref of hundred is supposed to correspond with a *Wapentake*, a division as in Yorkshire, because when the overlord appeared for justice, the men used to touch his spear, in token of feallg (*Wapen*, arms, and *tac*, to touch).

(†Penmaen Rhos in the Parish of Llysfaen).

‡Variously written thus "Rowaynok" "Rewynok" "Revoveanc," now called by the Welsh "Rhyfoniog" corruptly for "Rhiwoniog," *gwlad rhiwiau*, or *Rhiw-weunog*, signifying the hill country—the land of slopes and brows.

819, Egbert, king of the West Saxons, seized the lordship of Rhos Rhufoniog; about 1130 Gruffydd ap Cynan gave 10/- to the Church of Dinerth Goch Rufoniog"— so that the present Parish of Llandrillo-yn-Rhos was originally known as Dinerth or Dynerth or Denyryt.

In Myv. Archaiology there are four notices of St. Trillo :—

" Boneddy Saint "

" Trillo yn dinerth yn Rhos.
" Trillo yn Rhos ab Ithel o Lydaw.
" Terillo en Dinerth yn Rhos Mab Ithel o Lydaw.
" Trillo yn y ddinerth yn Rhos."

Anglicé.—The Pedigree of the Saint.

" Trillo in dinerth yn Rhos.
" Trillo yn Rhos ab Ithel o Lydan.
" Terillo in Dinerth yn Rhos, son of Ithel of Lydan.
" Trillo in the Dinerth yn Rhos."

It is therefore quite clear that the Parish of Llandrillo-yn-Rhos was originally known as Dynerth, Dinerth or Deneryt, probably from " Din-garth," i.e., the fort with earthworks.† The Ecclesiastical valor (value) or Taxation of Pope Nicholas IV. was made in or about 1291. In that Taxation of Pope Nicholas IV., the Rectorial (sinecure) value of the tithes was £15 6s. 8d. The Vicarial value of the tithes was £8 6s. 8d, this £8 6s. 8d. being made up of tenths :—

	£	s.	d.
On Grain and Hay	6	6	8
,, Lambs, Geese, Wool and	1	13	4
,, Little Pigs, Eggs	0	6	6
,, Glebe Lands	0	6	8
,, Personal Teythis, &c.	0	10	0
Total	9	3	2
Deduct for the Lord Bishop	0	16	6
	8	6	8

Under the Bishoprick of St. Asaph, in the Deanery of Rhos, Llandrillo-yn-Rhos or Dinerth was the Mother Church of an extensive district or Deanery embracing the surrounding parishes of Llanelian, Llansantffraid, Llan or Eglwys Rhos, and Llysfaen, in

†Professor Rhys, Principal of Jesus College, Oxford, in his presidential address at the Llandudno Eisteddfod, July 1896, suggested another derivation of " Dinerth." An extract from his address is given on a later page.

each of which it was the custom until about the end of the last century for the Vicar to preach two or four sermons annually, instead of which a money acknowledgment was substituted. There is no record concerning this Parish at any period from 1291 to 1535 (26th year of Henry VIII.), at which date the name of the Parish appears to have been changed from Dinerth or Dynerth to Llandrillo. In confirmation of this, I may mention that there is in the Parish Church a stone lid of a sarcophagus of Edneved which describes the Parish as Denyryt, but to this I shall have to refer more in detail later on. Llandrillo as it is now called—formerly Dinerth or Dynerth, is supposed to be the oldest Church in Wales. I may however here state that the present Parish Church was not the original Parish Church, but merely the private Chapel of the Feudal chief Edneved Vychan, who lived in the old ruins of Llŷs Euryn. It is generally spoken of even now as "yr hen furddyn "— i.e., the shell of an old building. As far as can be ascertained, the original Parish Church was situate about a mile and a half to East from Rhos Vynach and was built originally in that part of Dinerth Township which disappeared in the submergence of Morfa Rhiannedd, a large district that once stretched from the Great Orme's Head to beyond Abergele, and the Church was thence transferred to the present site on the application of the Parishioners to Edneved to enlarge his chapel eastward, and the bulge in the North Wall just below the new organ chamber clearly indicates the point from which it was lengthened.

I am gratefully indebted to the Rev. Meredith Hughes, St. Catherine's, Colwyn, for the following valuable information contained in his Notes, which, with his permission, I now insert:—

MORFA RHIANNEDD.

The first mention of the submerged district is in a short poem, A.D. 520, by Taliesin (Myv. Arch. 35), the most celebrated of British poets, Taliesin-Ben-Beirdd. He at one time dwelt on the banks of Llyn (Lake) Geirionydd, near Trefriw.

The whole poem was recited by Taliesin in Deganwy Castle, before Maelgwyn Gwynedd and thirty-three Bards.

It reads thus in Myvyrian Arch. :—

> Fe ddaw pry rhyfedd, o Forfa Rhiannedd
> I ddial anwiredd ar Vaelgwyn Gwynedd
> Ai flew, ai ddannedd, a'i lygaid yn eurydd
> A hyn a wna ddiwedd ar Vaelgwyn Gwynedd.

Anglicé :—" A strange creature will come from the Marsh of Rhiannedd, to punish the crimes of Maelgwyn Gwynedd : its hair, its teeth and its eyes are yellow, and this will destroy Maelgwyn Gwynedd."

The point of interest, of course, so far as it concerns the subject, is that the stanza mentions Morfa Rhiannedd.

II. Second mention in "Gorhoffet" Gwalchmai (Myv. Arch.), 1115—1190, again in connection with Maelgwyn Gwynedd.

"Morfa Rhiannedd Maelgwyn."

III. The third mention in the Welsh Triads, extracted from ancient MSS. by Thomas Jones, Tregaron, in 1601 : —

Three awful plagues of Britain : the second of which was the yellow pestilence of Rhos Rhiannedd.

IV. In Brut. G. ab Arthur (Myv. Arch.).

V. In Pennant's Tours in Wales : —

"There has always been a tradition or popular opinion that the original Abergele was overwhelmed by the sea, a calamity believed to have occurred about the 8th or 9th century. 'A stone tablet without a date, set in the Churchyard Wall, close to the North gate, is adduced as a proof of the inroads of the sea. This stone does not bear on the face of it any signs of great antiquity ; but there is a tradition among old people that the present one is only a copy of another of far more ancient date.' On the other side of the wall, there is to be seen a very old stone with portions of letters not now decipherable. This is held to be the original.

"The inscription on the stone at present in existence runs thus : —

' Yma mae'n gorwedd
Yn Mynwent Mihangel
Gwr oedd ei annedd
Dair milldir yn y Gogledd.'

"The English of which is : —

' Here lies
In the Churchyard of St. Michael
A man who had his residence
Three miles to the North.'

"The second line is evidently an interpolation. Leave this line out and you have something like the ancient Welsh verse, called 'Tribau Milwr '—'The Soldier's Triplet.' But might it not have been

' Yma mae'n gorwedd	.	' Here lies
Gwr oedd ei annedd		A man who had his residence
Yn Morfa Rhiannedd —		In Morfa Rhiannedd
Dair milldir i'r Gogledd.'		Three miles to the North,'

or the third line might have been the second, for Abergele undoubtedly stands in the Remnant of Morfa Rhiannedd, a coast plain which once stretched from the Point of Air in Flintshire, round Orme's Head to the Eastern Banks of the Conway."

Pennant further observes, that at low water a long tract of hard loam, far from the clayey bank, filled with bodies of oak trees tolerably entire, has been noticed. Trunks of trees may be seen even now at Rhos-on-Sea. It may be interesting to observe, as affording correlative evidence, that the large boulder, known as

Maen Rhys now under water, has a historic connection with this submerged district. According to the Cambrian Journal, Rhys was one of the well-known chief shepherds of Owain Gwynedd (1137) in this part of North Wales, and his custom was to blow his "hir-gorn bugeiliol" (shepherd's long horn) from this boulder. It would therefore appear that in the middle of the 12th century, a large tract remained unsubmerged, and within this unsubmerged territory would be Penmaenrhos, under which cliff, according to Pennant, Richard II. was taken prisoner. This agrees with a statement found in a curious French MS. in the British Museum, written by a French nobleman who accompanied Richard and was an eye-witness of the event. "We could not get away on one side owing to the sea, or on the other owing to the rock."

> "The dreadful ocean on the one side lay,
> The hard encroaching rock the other kept."
>
> *Civil Wars, Bk. I.*

O. Jones, in his History of Wales, quoting from an old Welsh Chronicle, says:—"If the Princes of Aberffraw and Powis should disagree, they were to meet by command of Rhodri their father (about 880) on Dôl Rhiannedd, and the Prince of Dinefwr, their brother, was authorised to mediate between them."

A provision was likewise made in the event of any disagreement between any two of these Princes.

Seithenyn Feddw was keeper of the Dyke, and tradition says that there were thirty gates in the Dyke between Gogarth and the Point of Air.

NOTES BY REV. MEREDITH J. HUGHES.

"Even now, sailors and fisher-folk declare that they can see the *Murian* or Walls—the Dyke or what remains of it. It is a matter of fact that the waves, at very low water, can be distinctly seen breaking in a long line from W. to E. about a mile from the shore.

Euryn was the son of Helig ap Glanawg, who after the submergence of Llys Helig, situated opposite Penmaenmawr, devoted himself to religion. He was known as Euryn y Coed Helig. He gave its name to Bryn Euryn. Tyno was another son of Helig, and probably lived at "Gwern Tyno," in this parish.

MAEN NAWDD.

In one of the fields near Glyn Fawr, there lies the remains of an immense Monolith, which I think must be of historical interest. It was at one time evidently in an upright position, and I venture to suggest, both from the nature and size of the stone, and also from the elevated position it occupied, that it was once a Maen Nawdd—a Rock of patronage or refuge—or Pillar of Safety. The stone pillars, mostly monoliths, marked the division of property and jurisdiction, something after the ancient Hebrew custom, mentioned *inter alia* in Genesis xxxi., a custom evidently derived from still more ancient nations. In Wales these were called Meini Crair—a forensic term, signifying Pillar of Covenant, on this account they were sometimes used as Benches of Justice, and if so, they were designated—white pillars or pillars of virtue. Towards the end of the Feudal period, an offender against the Law could fly to one of these and claim the protection of the lord in whose district it was situated. Thus the Maen Nawdd was to a certain extent a City of Refuge ; at all events it afforded the fugitive a right of sanctuary. The position of this Monolith, erected on an elevated spot, would render it visible for a long distance, and it divided the jurisdiction of Gloddaeth from that of Brynffanigl.

Cassell's Concise Cyclopædia gives a definition of a sanctuary or place of refuge, as a place where criminals and debtors might shelter themselves from justice, and from which they could not be taken without sacrilege. Temples and altars were asylums : as were also tombs, statues and monuments. In modern times, the extent of the privilege of sanctuary or asylum was matter of violent dispute between the Church and the Civil power. It was only by an Act of Parliament passed in 1534, after the Reformation, that persons accused of treason were debarred from the privilege of sanctuary. After the complete establishment of the Reformation, in the reign of Elizabeth, neither the churches nor sanctuaries of any other description were allowed to be any longer places of refuge for criminals. In 1697, all such sanctuaries or asylums, even for debtors, were finally suppressed."

A little higher up the glen (Nant y Glyn Valley) on a farm called Bryn y Maen, there is an interesting old ruin and *Well* called Ffrith St. Crysto. Very little is known of this Saint. He is either Cristiolus, son of Ynys of Britany, mentioned in Myv. Archai., or Crysto, a saint of Ireland who came to this part of Wales about the same time as St. Beuno, early in the seventh century. Or it may have been St. Crwst, a saint of the sixth century, contemporary with Maelgwyn Gwynedd.

This Crwst, with St. Trillo and Deiniol, Bishop of Bangor, signed a document under the authority of the King—Maelgwyn Gwynedd—granting certain rights, ecclesiastical and other privileges, to St. Cyndeyrn (Kentigern), the founder of the see of St. Asaph.

TWR JIWBILI (Jubilee Tower).

Beyond Brynymaen, at the extreme South corner of the Parish, are to be seen the remains of a Tower, erected like the larger one at Moel Fammau, on the Vale of Clwyd Mountains, in 1810, to commemorate the Jubilee of George III. It is said to have been from twenty-five to thirty feet high, but, judging by the circumference of the base, it could not have been above ten or fifteen high. It was built partly of peat, partly of sods upon a base of unprepared stones.

TIR Y BRENIN (King's land).

It is not at all remarkable to find stretches of unenclosed lands here and there called Tir y Goron, or Crown Lands. But with the exception of the single instance of Tir y Brenhin, a joint hamlet with Briskedwin, in the Parish of Llandelio, near Swansea, this, so far as I know, is the only piece of land so called. It retains the name by which it was known long before the conquest of Wales, and the Charter of Rhuddlan. I have been told that the Office of Woods and Forests know nothing of it ; it is certain that no tithe is paid on it—the extent comprised being about 400 acres.

MYNYDD MERCI

is at the top end of the Parish on the confines of Llansantffraid ; possibly so called from *Mercuri*—Mercury—whom the Romans worshipped—a Cultus (worship) introduced by them into Wales."

The Rev. Meredith J. Hughes has most kindly given me the following particulars of a remarkable discovery he has very recently made of the traces of a British Camp at Mynydd Merci in this Parish. I quote in full his own description :—

"The ancient Welsh regarded Brutus, a Prince of Troy, as the original founder of their nation. It is very curious to note that they sought to propitiate their tradition by cutting a plan of Ilium, the chief city of Troy, in the greensward and on mountain sides. The Welsh for Ilium is Caerdroia—The City of Troy, and it is conjectured that the suffix—droia, which means to *circle*, suggested to them the interesting plan showing in the accompanying diagram. These plans of Ilium were very common in the Principality some few centuries ago. The second diagram shows the remains of one of these mazes and may be seen at Mynydd Merci, about a mile to the S.W. of the New Church now being built by Mrs. Frost at Brynymaen. I have previously traced here the lines of an extensive British hill-camp, and my conjecture is that some of these lines were made use of in delineating the geometrical design of Ilium. It is to be regretted that the lines cannot be accurately traced owing to various causes, chiefly the fact that much of the land is under cultivation."

LLETTY'R DRYW.

There is on the road to Colwyn Village a small Farm called Lletty'r Dryw. This is probably mentioned by Owain Kyveilianc, a Prince-poet (1130—1197), Myv. Arch.,

> " Ac annwny y rôs nosweith."
> " We shall rest a night at Rhos,"

meaning a recognised Inn, or staying place. Lletty'r Dewrion—encampment of soldiers on the march.

After this digression, which I trust my readers will consider pardonable, I must now revert to the description of the interior of Llandrillo Church.

In the North Wall of the old Feudal Chapel (the present Church) there are to be seen two arches which communicated with Edneved's family seat, under which was the cemetery, where he was afterwards buried ; his dependants occupied the space to the South of the family seat. This private Chapel was originally built under Licence of the Pope for evermore to sing Divine Service therein for his soul and his ancestors and progenitors for ever, and had authority " to give his tithes and oblations to his chaplain there serving."

The present old Church is prettily situated on an eminence which commands a charming view of the surrounding picturesque country. I always consider that it is a view unsurpassed from any Church-yard in the Kingdom, combining as it does at a glance every feature that enhances the beauty of a landscape. The North aisle of the Church was erected in the 13th century. The South aisle was built in the 15th century by the Ladies Conwy, the descendants of Gruffydd Goch, Lord of Rhos and Rhyfoniog and collaterally of Edneved Vychan ; they were the last occupiers of the Llys (Court of Bryn Euryn). They also left a large sum of money towards restoring the present handsome Tower. The church is a substantial-looking edifice with a massive square tower which possesses some peculiar features such as loop lights with ogee heads, with a stair in the S.W. angle over which rises a " look out " or watch-place. This ancient Church fulfilled as many duties as in old times the Cathedral of St. Andrews, being a temple of religion, a place of observing the approach of foes, and a fortress if attacked.

The battlements are stepped in the Irish fashion, and as at Llanbeblig, near Carnarvon, and nowhere else in North Wales. There are, I believe, several in Ireland. The two aisles are separated by four arches of the late perpendicular period, and the carved stone angel-corbels at their spring indicate that they were intended for a roof much more elaborate than the present plain one of oak. That of the N. aisle is of a plan rarely found in churches of this date, but much adopted in the present day. The main beams of the principals in the S. aisle have a tie-beam at more than half their altitude, and athwart this beam two springers or subsidiary beams, starting half-way down between the tie-beam and the top of the wall, run up, cross each other above the tie-beam, and then fasten themselves into the principals. A series of three quadrilaterals above three triangles is thus formed, all strongly pegged together, light in appearance, and sufficiently rigid to have stood for several centuries.

The two East windows, now filled with beautiful stained glass, are one of four lights,* the other of three lights,† and similar in design to those of Whitchurch, near Denbigh, and many others of the same period.‡ The Font is an octagonal basin of Early English date, and has a beading of the tooth ornament around the rim, and is quite perfect.

There is a Piscina in the South chancel§; and an Ambry in the East wall of the N. aisle.‖

The Lych (Corpse) Gate has the following inscription :—

†* HENRY : VAIGHAN

OWEN : WILLIAMS

Wardens.

Ano: Domini

1677

M. R.

Charles II. was King, and Robert Foulkes was Vicar. He was Vicar Choral St. Asaph 1665 ; appointed Vicar of this Parish in 1666.

What is the meaning of M.R. ? I venture to suggest that it is " Mortui resurgent,"—" The dead shall rise again."

---

*Representing the Crucifixion (Heaton, Butler & Bayne).

†The Nativity (Barraud & Westlake).

‡The S.E. window – The Resurrection (Heaton, Butler & Bayne).

The S. window The Ascension (Heaton, Butler & Bayne).

§Piscina, a basin near the Altar, into which the priest empties the water used in the service ; it is often the only remaining indication of the place where an altar has been. (Latin, A fish-pond).

Ambry or Almonry, a place where alms are deposited for distribution ; a niche near the altar for the sacred vessels ; a cupboard.

†*This was Henry Vaughan of Glyn. The following sketch of plaster from a loft in Glyn Farm is interesting : —

The Church, after having been restored under the supervision of Mr. Kennedy (Bangor) during the incumbency of my predecessor (Rev. Thomas Hughes), was re-opened on the 3rd of September, 1857, and is seated for 350. An organ was built by Hill & Son, London, in 1874, at a cost of £215, and was first placed in the space near to the door leading to the Tower. It was removed in 1875 to the present organ chamber, built for the purpose at a cost of £150. The organ was enlarged in 1895 by Connacher & Son (Huddersfield), at a cost of £350.

I must not forget to mention St. Trillo Chapel, near the Weir on the shore, which was built by Maelgwyn Gwynedd about the sixth century. It is specially interesting, from being a unique specimen of those oratories which formed the type of the earliest British Churches, and corresponds to the primitive oratories of Ireland and Cornwall. There is at the East end a perennial spring, where it is supposed the first Missionary baptised his converts, and whence the water for Baptism in the several Churches of the Parish in succeeding ages was religiously borne. Occasionally a cell or oratory such as this, has kept alive through many vicissitudes the name of an early—if not the earliest Evangelist of the place.

This ancient oratory of St. Trillo is in form a Parallelogram, about 15 feet long by 8 feet wide, the East end and both sides being pierced with loopholes or lancets. The roof is vaulted and consists of small stones. It has lately been restored by Mr. William Horton, the present owner of the Rhos Fynach Estate.

*The Bishop and the Vicar of the Parish are entitled to the Tithe of Fish taken in the Weir every tenth day from May 13th to October 18th, and the owner of the Weir in former times, insisted on continuing an immemorial custom of having prayers read in this chapel three times during the fishing season—"as it was customary on all sea coasts in these parts, when tithes of fish were paid." I have been told that this custom is still kept up on the West Coast of Ireland. In illustration of Capel Trillo, Rev. Elias Owen, F.S.A., Vicar of Llanyblodwell, near Oswestry, says :— "Near the mouth of the Ogwen was formerly a 'Capel Ogwen,' where the fishermen's boats were blessed before they set out to sea. The old chapel has been superseded by a new building, in which Lord Penrhyn's keeper lives."

* In former times, up to 1872, the Bishop of St. Asaph had three-fourths, and the Vicar of Llandrillo one-fourth of the Tithe of Fish taken every tenth day. from May 13th to October 18th. It is a remarkable fact, that twelve out of twenty-five Cathedrals are built on Salmon Rivers.

BLESSING THE FIELDS.

Exract from " Social Hours with Celebrities," by the late Mr.
W. Pitt Byrne, being 3rd and 4th Vols. " Gossip of the Century."

"Mr. Waterton belonged to a great old English family. The pages of
Doomsday Book testify that the Waterton family is one of the oldest in the
Kingdom. Mr. Waterton's seat was Walton, near Wakefield, a great stone
mansion, which stands on arches in the midst of a lake of thirty or forty acres,
and successfully stood a siege from Cromwell himself. Mr. Charles Waterton,
when he settled down after his wanderings in South America, would not allow
any birds to be killed or molested. Another of his hobbies was to maintain
ancient religious customs, such as—Blessing the Fields. ' The ancient Catholic
custom had always been kept up by the family at Walton, without intermission,
from time immemorial of the annual blessing of the fields.' . . . . The priest,
preceded by the processional cross bearer, and attended by two acolytes in
scarlet cassocks and short white cottas, walked first, aspersing the soil and
chanting the Rogation litanies, the responses being taken up by those who
followed. The little procession took its winding way round the farm lands,
passing through here and there a copse or a clump of trees, from behind which
it might be seen now and again emerging, or crossing a bridge, or gently
sweeping round some farm building ; the voices, as they chanted, floating on
the air with a unison which told of the earnestness and sympathy of all.
Immediately behind the priest walked the squire bareheaded, and wearing his
goodly eighteenth century costume, and heading his family and household,
these being followed by the farm labourer and the Catholic villagers, delighted
with the privilege of being associated in the pious rite."

Connected with the foregoing most interesting ceremony, I give
below an extract from the *Daily Mail*, May 16th, 1898 :—

PRAYING FOR THE CROPS.

INTERESTING REVIVAL OF AN OLD CUSTOM.

Yesterday being the fifth Sunday after Easter, otherwise known as Rogation
Day, and a period for special supplication, the curious old custom of "praying
for the crops" was duly observed at Hitchin, an old-fashioned market town,
some thirty miles from London, a district famous for its lavender and for its
nightingales.

At half-past two in the afternoon a procession, headed by one of the choir
carrying a cross and the choristers and clergy, wearing their surplices, left the
Church of St. Saviour, singing the hymn, "Our Blessed Redeemer, ere
He Breathed," and wended its way through the streets towards the fields and
homesteads in the Walsworth and Purwell districts, and when near to the
church appropriate hymns and prayers were offered up for a blessing upon the
the crops.

Standing in a framework of delicate greenery, the choir and clergy, together
with the many members of the congregation and others who had joined in the
procession, made the pastoral service an impressive one, the singing of the
hymns being very heartily performed. Propitious weather favoured the
ceremony, the heat being oppressive.

To-day the choir and clergy of St. Mary's Church, situated in another
portion of the town, will visit the neighbouring districts of the parish, and
offer up similar prayers and hymns.

The revival of this old custom in North Herts has now been observed annually for several years.

After the copious rains of the past few weeks the young corn is just now looking extremely well, and the farmers' hearts are already gladdened by the sight of some eight inches to twelve inches of healthy growth, strong in the blade and of a very good colour; indeed, throughout Herts, as in other districts, the present season promises to be one of the most fruitful on record, both in field and orchard.

"BLESSING THE HARVEST FIELDS."
(*Vide* LORNA DOONE, Chap. 29.)

The Golden Harvest came, waving on the broad hill-side. All the parish was assembled in our upper Courtyard, for we were to open the harvest that year. We started in proper order; first the parson, Josiah Bowden, wearing his gown and cassock, with the Parish Bible in his hand, and a sickle strapped behind him. When we were come to the big field gate, where the first sickle was to be, Parson Bowden heaved up the rail with the sleeves of his gown done green with it, and he said that everybody might hear him, " In the name of the Lord, Amen ! "

" Amen, so be it," cried the Clerk.

Then Parson Bowden read some verses from the Parish Bible, letting us to lift up our eyes, and look upon the fields already white to harvest : and then he laid his Bible down on the square head of the gate-post, and despite his gown and cassock, three good stripes he cut of corn and laid them right end onwards. When he had stowed the corn like that —we said —" Thank the Lord for all His mercies, and these the first fruits of His hand ! " And then the Clerk gave out a Psalm, verse by verse. And the Psalm was sung so strongly that the foxgloves on the bank were shaking, like a chime of bells."

Having referred at sufficient length to the archæology of the ancient and interesting Church, a more detailed account of the history of Edneved Vychan now claims our attention. He was the son of Cynan ab Ior. ab Gwgan ab Marchudd, and had his principal residence in the Creuddyn District, at Llys Euryn*. Llys Euryn was formerly called Maelgwyn Gwynedd ; Maelgwyn had his residence herein in the 6th century, whereas Edneved inhabited it about the 13th century.

Edneved was Prime Minister to Llewelyn ap Iorwerth ; he was descended from Maredudd ab Cynan, chief of one of the Tribes of North Wales.† He wore upon his breast-plate in the first instance

---

* Lewis (Topographical Wales II.) says, that Llys Euryn was burnt down in 1409 by Owain Glyndwr, but the remains were modernised, and were occupied by the Ladies Conwy, descendants of Sir Tudur ab Edneved. This Sir Tudur was one of the Commissioners for negotiating terms of peace between Edward I. and Llewelyn.

†He died 1136, and was buried on the left side of the great altar at Bangor. Amongst other legacies to churches, he bequeathed 10s. to the Parish of Dineth (Llandrillo) and many other principal churches ; in fact, we are told that during his time North Wales glittered with churches as the Firmament with stars. *Yorke's Royal Tribes of Wales.*

LLANDRILLO-YN-RHOS CHURCH.

—' A Saracen's Head'—which indicated that he or some of his ancestors had been in the War of the Cross, or the Crusades, the first of which was in 1096. In reference to the Crusades, I may here mention that in 1288 Pope Nicholas IV granted the tenths to King Edward the First for six years towards defraying the expenses of an expedition to the Holy Land. A new feature resulting from the Crusades is from that time not infrequently met with in the St. Asaph Diocesan records, viz., the introduction of leprosy into the country, e.g., "duodecim leprosarii" (twelve lepers) receive clothing from Bishop Llewelyn A.D. 1311, and there was at Wrexham a "terra leprosorum" (a region of lepers). There was once a terrible battle between the Welsh under Edneved Vychan and the Saxons (English) under Ranulph, Earl of Chester. Edneved succeeded in conquering his enemies and slew also three of their chief officers, for which his Prince commanded him thenceforward to wear upon his breast-plate "Gules between three Englishmen's heads (triphen Sais) couped and Chevron Ermine "— which distinguishes his descendants up to the present time.

Edneved was twice married, 1st, to a daughter of Llyerch ap Bran, by whom, among other children, he had Hywel, Bishop of St. Asaph. One of his officers was Gruffydd Llwyd of Dregarnedd (Anglesey), who was created a knight by Edward I., for conveying when at Rhuddlan Castle the news of the birth of his heir, Edward II., first Prince of Wales, in Carnarvon Castle. 2nd, to Gwenllian, daughter of Rhys, Prince of South Wales. Gwenllian is the lady commonly styled the heiress of Dyffryn Clwyd. The meaning of Gwenllian is white linen, the lady being remarkable not only for her beauty but also for her personal cleanliness, a quality which in that age, when linen was scanty and soap did not exist, must have been even more attractive than it is at present. Linen was so rare in the reign of Charles VII. of France, who lived about the time of Henry VI. (1450), that the Queen of France could boast of two shifts only of that commodity.— *Yorke's Royal Tribes of Wales.*

Many causes of animosity subsisted between Edward, Llewelyn, and the Welsh, previous to the final rupture. In the year 1277, the Barons of Snowdon, with other noblemen of Wales, had attended Llewelyn to London, when he came thither at Christmas to do homage to Edward, for the four Cantrefs (Hundreds) of Rhôs, Rhyfoniog (that is, Denbigh), Tegengl, and another in Dyffryn Clwyd, and bringing, according to their usual custom, large retinues with them, were quartered at Islington and the neighbouring villages. These places did not afford milk for such numerous trains; they liked neither the wine nor the ale of London ; and though plentifully entertained, were much displeased at the new manner of living, which did not suit their taste ; they slighted the English bread, and their pride too was disgusted by the perpetual staring of the Londoners, who followed them in crowds to gaze at their uncommon garb. "No," cried the indignant Britons, "we never again will visit Islington except as conquerors," and from that instant they resolved to take up arms. *From a MS. in the Mostyn Collection.*

†100 Villages.— A Cantref contained fifty townships, and a Commot or Cwmmwd was the third of a Cantref. From Cwmmwd we derive Cymmydog, a neighbour.

The Sovereigns of North Wales preserved their title of Princes till 1282, on the death of the last Llewelyn. The kingly title ended with Gruffydd ab Cynan.— *Yorke's Royal Tribes.*

There were twenty-one Lords Marchers, who sat among the English Lords, and had the titles of those places they had won from the Welsh. They had originally legal jurisdiction in their several Baronies, where the King's writ did not run. This was intended as a strength against the neighbouring enemy, but Edward the First, in his Statute of Rhuddlan, withdrew this power, for he was able of himself to rule our countrymen. None were elected after that period; they held of the King immediately and were accordingly bound to him in personal suit and service and to find him a certain number of soldiers. In the third of Edward the Second, for the Scotch War, the Barony of Rhos and Rhyfoniog had to send two hundred; Ruthin two hundred; Dyffryn Clwyd one hundred; numbers exceeding the present Militia proportions. There can be little doubt from these comparative proportions that the neighbourhood had considerably more inhabitants than it hath at present, many as in these times being necessarily drawn off by trade and other engagements.— *Yorke's Royal Tribes.*

Edneved was absent from home for several years, connected with which there is an old Welsh Poem, entitled, " Ffarwel Edneved Fychain" (Edneved Vychan's Farewell), and a very interesting legend it is. It runs thus:—" Edneved went off on a warlike expedition, leaving behind him Gwenllian and the children at Llys Euryn, and on leaving he composed and played a tune of Farewell to his Gwenllian. He was absent for many years, till his wife believed that he was dead, and accepted the offer of a gentleman who came forward to ask for her hand. But on the night of the wedding there came to the door a beggar, pitiable to look at—to ask for a morsel and a night's lodging; and after he ascertained what was going on, and receiving permission to go in as a player to amuse the company, he asked for the " loan of the old harp that was there formerly." Having repaired the harp he struck up the old Tune, ' Edneved Vychan's Farewell,' and before he reached the tenth stanza, the wedding festivities were over—the wife and her husband were approaching the door for their honeymoon. Edneved, raising his hand from the harp, exclaimed :—

' Os bum ar ffo, dro yn druan gwallus
I'm golli Gwenllian !
Ni chollaf,—ewch chwi allan —
Na gwely—na thŷ na thân ! ' "

I make no apology for here introducing a very pretty Ballad, entitled, "The Home Coming of Edneved Vychan," written by a British matron (Mrs. Watts Jones), a frequent visitor to Rhos-on-Sea.

THE HOME-COMING OF EDNEVED VYCHAN.

A gray old church and a gray old stone,
　　Down by the western sea,
Some loopholed walls with ivy grown,
And one gray tower that stands alone,
　　And a tale that was told to me.

Once the warrior's banner flew
　　Where the rose and the bramble twine ;
Once the warder's war-horn blew
　　Where low the large-eyed kine ;
And where linnet and throstle and blackbird sing,
Once the minstrel's harp did ring.

Rampart and buttress are overthrown,
But the church stands firm, and the gray old stone,
And carving and blazon lie buried in weed,
But on the stone you a line may read,
　　" Hic jacet Dominus Edneved."

I.

The autumn day was closing in,
　　Gray vapours hid the sun,
The waves dashed up with an angry din,
　　The clouds hung low and dun,
And the fisherman hard by St. Seiriol's shrine
Hauled up his boat and drew in his line.

II.

And 'twixt the sea and the mountain brown
　　A palmer he went his way,
Last even a caravel set him down,
A caravel trading from Genoa town,
　　For copper, to Amlwch Bay.

III.

" Thou knowest the sea and thou knowest the hour,"
　　He to the fisherman cried,
" Can I pass round the spur of Penmaenmawr .
　　In the teeth of the rising tide ?
For low on the hills the rain-clouds lower,
　　And by Conway this night I bide."

IV.

" If firm and fleet be thy sandall'd feet,"
　　The fisherman he 'gan say,
" Ere the flood-tide flow thou may'st safely go,
　　And land thee in Penmaen bay ;
But yet are thy perils not overpast,
Round Penmaenbach the flood-tide swirls fast,

And wolves are in Dwygyfylchi glen,
And the Sychnant is held by Cochwillan's men ;
  Ah ! filled is the land with dule and tyne
Sin' mine old lord tarries in Palestine ! "
" Grammercy for thy news, good friend,
  Soon may St. Seiriol thy troubles end ;
  But as gold may endanger my way, now take
This guerdon of me for thine old lord's sake ;
  And pray thou Our Lady that of her sweet grace
She bring him in peace to his resting place."
The fisherman stood amazed, I ween
'Twas the first gold bezant he e'er had seen.

The palmer he plunged in the scud and spray,
And quickly he came into Penmaen bay,
Then away he strode over hill and glen,
With the swinging step of the mountain men ;
Blithely he breasted the steep Sychnant,
Where path there was none, and the light was scant ;
Cochwillan's men heard as they lay below,
But they deemed it the rush of some frighted roe,
Then with slackened knees he dropped adown
The long dun ridge into Conway town.

VII.

The North wind blustered up Conway bay,
But soft on his cheek was the drifting spray,
And sweet the sound of the grating oar,
And the scent of the seaweed on the shore,
And the rise and fall of the ferry-man's speech,
And the crash of the bow on the shingle beach,—
The drops on his cheek were not all sea form
For now at last he was nearing home.

VIII.

He has found the old woodland track again,
And little recked he of the wind and rain ;
The splash of the rain made his ear rejoice,
The swell of the wind was an old friend's voice,
The scented willow-herb brushed his path,
The meadows were sweet with the aftermath.
And a startled thrush from the brake sang clear,
" Edneved, Edneved, Edneved is here !"

IX.

Seven years agone, with a gallant band,
    He had ridden along that way,
And those years seemed a story written in sand,
    That the waves had just washed away,
But the day he quitted his native land
    It might have been yesterday ;
When the anchors were weighed with a joyous clang,
And pennons fluttered and trumpets rang,
And priests the " Veni Creator " sang,
    As they sailed from Carnarvon bay.

X.

For the banner of Christ was on the wind,
    And the Vicar of Christ the war proclaimed,
And who was the caitiff would stay behind
    To be for ever shamed?
Not he, forsooth, Llewelyn's best man,
    Lord of the Marches, Edneved Vychan.

XI.

Long with the English had he warred
    Ere the call from across the sea,
He had splintered lance and had dinted sword
    With the flower of their chivalry :
But when the third Henry was on the throne
England had trouble eno' of her own.

XII.

Now all that in the crusade befell
Is written far better than I can tell
    By the Seneschal of Champagne ;*
A noble tale of a noble life,
That shines like a star o'er the sickening strife
    Of those ages of guilt and pain.
Who in life's battle is ready to faint,
Let him take courage from Louis the Saint.

XIII.

At last 'twas finished. The march by night,
    The Greek fire darting athwart the sky,
The nacaire's clang in the dawning light,
The burning shafts from the noontide height,
    When the strongest sicken and die ;
The maddening dance of the hot red air,
    The blinding blaze of the hot white plain,
The desolate watch on some outpost bare,
    The fury that surges o'er nerve and brain
    When the friend you love at your side is slain
All—all had sunk in that fathomless sea,
    That fathomless sea without a shore
That gulfs things mortal and craves for more,
    Men call it " Eternity."

XIV.

Could it be true he was home again?
The moon shone out through the mist and rain,
And silvered the pine ridge of woody Pabo;
Dark lay the meadows and stream below ;
And the woods were unscathed from their birth to death
The meadows they feared not the Sirocco's breath,
And the waters they ran, not to ban, but to bless :
And the valley seemed fashioned by God's caress,
And the little hills framed to bring righteousness.

---

*See the " Memoirs of the Count de Joinville."

XV.

Yes, it was true he was home again,
  Home again in his own countree !
He plucked the wet fruit from the bramble tree,
And touched a nettle and loved the sting,
For a sudden thought made his pulses spring,
  " The babes and I will go blackberrying !"

XVI.

His own loved babes and his own sweet wife !
Never before in all his life
  Had he known how he loved them all ;
One short hour and they would be
Safe in his arms and about his knee,
  In his own Bryn Eyron's hall.
And he sang the song that he once had sung
In the scented spring when the world was young.

EDNEVED'S SONG TO THE LADY GWENLLIAN AP RHYS, WHO BECAME
HIS WIFE.

I.

The moon stands afar o'er the crags of high Bryn Eyre,
  And the voice of the streamlet wakes, and hush'd is the wind's wild roll,
And my love shines afar o'er the summit of my desire,
  And the roar of life is stilled, and wakes the song o' the soul.
Beautiful is my love, and born in a beautiful land,
  Where bright flashes the sea in the smile of the sun's glad shine,
Where fair are forest and field, and steadfast the mountains stand,
  But fairer than aught in land or sea is the smile of her eyes in mine !

2.

She wanders afield at morn, and a myriad songs rejoice !
  A myriad flowers fling their sweets on the wayward air,
And the dappled fawn is held by the call of her gentle voice,
  And the startled leveret stays beholding a thing so fair,
While softly the cloudlet sleeps on the summit of Siabod's crest,
  And right on Mellynlynn's lake falls the thistledown white and fine
And softly ripples the wave as it kisses the tern's white breast —
  But softer than cloud, or down, or wave, is the touch of her lips on mine !

3.

Like spray from the mountain stream falls her laugh on the sunlit air
  Silent and certain her step, as the step of the moon on the height ;
Like the curl of the wave at eve is the flow of her shining hair,
  She enters a darkened room, and lo ! it is filled with light.
White gleam her small hands like stars in the dusky heather,
  Lithe is she as the alder, straight as the tallest pine,
And the sound of her voice is sweet as the cooing of doves together,
  But sweeter than aught in earth or heaven is the beat of her heart on mine

XVII.

Now he was climbing the wind-swept knowe,
From whence his home he would see below,
 Dark in the dim moonlight ;
The castle, he knew, would be buried in sleep,
But the warder his faithful watch would keep,
 In the hush of the silent night ;
For the wind had sunk, and the land was still,
And the sheep they slept on the fern-clad hill,
And only the breath of the slumbering sea
Rose and fell in a lullaby.

XVIII.

He has gained the knowe.--What makes him stare
And start and grasp at the empty air ?
 The castle all dazzling shone ;
And over the silent night was borne,
The clang of harp, and the clash of horn,
 To the hill where he stood alone.

XIX.

Down he hurried and smote the gate,
" What ho ! my friend, now why so late,
 Do your gentles feast or fray ?
Llewelyn the Prince, doth he here abide,
And to him is gathered the country side ?
 Tell me your news, I pray ! "

XX.

" Come in, come in, be thou greatest or least,
For guests they are thronging from west and from east,
And welcome are all to the marriage feast,"
 The warder he gaily said,
" For Gwenllian, our dame of the shining hand,
The loveliest lady in Powysland —
 This morn was our lady wed."

XXI.

" Since ye are keeping the wedding feast,
 I am come on a lucky day ;
A palmer I from the Holy Land,
No gift or grace bear I in my hand,
 And here I must not stay ;
But hie to thy lady and pray that she
Will lend me a harp, if a harp there be,
 And I'll sing her a marriage lay."

XXII.

A blow, that shivers the life in twain
May by a brave man as a jest be ta'en,
And tongue will find the right words to say,
Though heart and brain be as soulless clay ;
But while the warder his message bore
He stood in the shadow beyond the door,

And the ground beneath him grew vague and dim,
And wife, home, lands, vanished far away,
And a langour stole over heart and limb,
And him seemed   he was lying as once he lay,
Weary and wounded among the slain ;
And the full moon rose over Ascalon plain,
Where the crescent had flamed through an angry day —
And gleamed on turban and scimitar,
And gray, still faces upturned to her ;
Faces *how* calm in the pale green light !
And he thought " Would my heart were as theirs this night."

XXIII.

" My lady she bids thee here abide
   And rest thee until the morning tide,
   And eat of her meat, and drink of her wine,
   For well she loves palmers from Palestine ;
   And when thou refresh'st and rested be,
   A marriage lay she will crave of thee."

XXIV.

Down he sank in the doorway seat,
And they brought him wine, and they brought him meat,
And he gazed up the lofty hall.
Yes ! There she sat in her carven chair,
Paler, it might be ; but ah ! how fair,
And near her was many a damsel rare,
But she was the flower of all.

XXV.

And minstrels and jongleurs thronged around,
And gaily did story and jest rebound,
And the hall was filled with a joyous sound :
And the lights flashed high, and the wine poured red,
But his heart in his bosom was heavy as lead,
And he felt like one who had long been dead.

None spake to him and he spake to none,
In the home of his longing he sat alone ;
Every rafter and stone he knew,
Each loopholed niche where the moon smiled through,
Each stain and chink in the rush-strewn floor,
Each notch in the beam that barred the door ;
His harp where it hung on the inner wall —
How oft in his dreams he had seen it all !
How oft in the anguish of fever dire
He had thought " All were well by mine own hall fire
And the fitful breathing would sink in peace,
And the throb in the knotted temples cease,
As the vision like blessed truth would seem,
Now, truth was but as a ghastly dream.

XXVI.

Then, slowly, athwart his wearied brain
The thoughts came back, and each thought was pain.
There sat the bridegroom, fair and fine,
He knew him—the heir of Maredydd's line ;
If he should rend him limb from limb,—
What would that serve if she grieved for him ?
If he should greet her and dare his fate,—
Could he endure if her love were hate ?
Should he hide his head in some convent bare,
And raise the psalm and intone the prayer,
And leave his wife to this stranger's kiss ?
—God, had he lived but for this, *for this ?*

XXVII.

" Come, haste thee, good palmer, the night draws on,
The bridegroom is bidding the guests begone ;
Long has he waited his lady's grace,
See'st thou the blush on her winsome face ?
Come haste thee and sing them a rousing lay
That luck may be theirs e'er the break of day ! "

XXVIII.

The warder's words like a whip-cord stung ;
Now hand me yon harp on the wall is hung,
And though joints be stiffened and voice long changed,
And hope departed and love estranged,
I'll sing them a song of the days gone by,
When women could love—if men must die."

XXIX.

'Tis said that he sang the last " farewell "
He had sung when he went on pilgrimage ;
But how can an alien rhymester tell
The notes of that strange, melodious age,
When music and words were wont to twine
Like briony growing with eglantine ;
Seek in the murmur of wind and sea
The sound of that silent minstrelsy.

XXX.

EDNEVED'S FAREWELL.

Written to an adaptation of the old Welsh Air, " Tros y Garcg."

I.

The call has come from beyond the main,
Brief our parting if long our pain,
Silent the harpstring when sorrow is sorest,
Blithely we'll sing when we meet again.
God, He wills it ! Flash bright my sword !
Fierce and strong is the Paynim horde.
Who but a coward would tarry at home
When infidels hold the home of his Lord ?

2.

The salmon he knows his path in the sea,
The twint he returns to his own oak tree,
The curlew seeketh the same crag-side,
But who can tell where my path shall be ?
God, He wills it ! Away, away,
Be it death to go, it were shame to stay,
Death is the seal of the lover's true loving,
Shame were death to our love for aye.

3.

Fret not for what is beyond recall,
Fear not, whatsoever befall,
Fear is for cowards and comes of the devil,
Death is God's mercy lighting on all.
God, He wills it ! Farewell, my son,
Guard thine honour as I have done,
Farewell, my Gwenllian, my life, my heart's treasure,
Though waters divide us, in love we are one.

XXXI.

The first few notes fell faint and slow,
Like a passing bell when a life runs low ;
The next flew free and fresh and high,
Like a bugle call when the foe is nigh ;
Then a storm of sound crashed over the hall
Like the roar of the winds when the pinewoods call
And blind blasts whip up the blistering foam,
And the boat is swamped as she runs for home.

XXXII.

It ceased, and silence fell on the clan.
    Sudden, the bridegroom sprang to his feet,
" A wedding lay *this*, thou holy man ?
    For a funeral dirge it were far more meet ;

XXXIII.

" Sing us a song for our honeymoon."
    But the bride spoke not, nor stirred in her place,
But her breath came quick to her heart's quick tune,
    And the red and the white hurried over her face.

XXXIV.

Boldly he strode up the sounding hall,
    Never a word to the groom spake he.
Heeded not churchman, or kinsman, or thrall,
    " Gwenllian, then hast thou forsaken me ? "

XXXV.

Edneved Vychan he is dead and gone,
    Sadly I mourned him many a year."
" Then are the days of thy mourning done,
    Edneved Vychan,—he standeth here ! "

XXXVI.

" If thou, indeed, be my long lost lord,
  Bend thy head lower, that I may see
Thine ear, that was scarred by the Norman sword,
  When thou drovest their horsemen beyond the Dee."

XXXVII.

His pilgrim's cowl he hath cast aside,
He hath bent his head till it touched her knee,
And she felt the scar, where the helmet tried
  Was cloven in twain on the Banks o' Dee.

XXXVIII.

" God's teeth," swore the bridegroom in angry scorn,
  " What care I who the varlet be ?
Wedded wast thou to me this morn,
  And after seven years a woman is free."

XXXIX.

Silent and trembling she waited there,
  Silent Edneved he eyed the twain,
Then he flung himself down in the bridegroom's chair,
  And clashed on his harp in a different strain.

XL.

*" A wanderer I, and aweary of strife,
  Get ye gone if ye so desire,
But if I may not have my own wife
  I'll have my own bed, my own house, my own fire ! "

  Os bym ar ffo, dro yn druan—gwallus
    I'm golli Gwenllian !
  Ni chollaf,—ewch chwi allan,
  Na gwely, na thŷ, na thân !

XLI.

Softly she turned, and a laugh laughed she,
  " Ever wast thou a masterful man,
But one lord at once is enough for me,
  And I'll be the wife of Edneved Vychan."
  * * * * * * *

XLII.

Long they lived in Bryn Euryn's hall,
  Sons and daughters she bore him there,
Sons who were sturdy and truthful and tall,
  Daughters loving and fair.
And kind was Edneved to rich and poor,
  And pilgrims and minstrels thronged his door ;
The church he built, where to-day it stands,
  And gave it rich cornfields and pasture lands.

* The original of this verse has been preserved.
  * * * * * * *

XLIII.

And every morn, so the chroniclers say,
  A story, I wis, recorded of few—
Edneved he went to the church, to pray
  For his ancestors, and his descendants too.

XLIV.

Were his prayers answered? Who can tell?
Since he was laid in his narrow cell,
In the gray old church 'neath the gray old stone,
Nigh on seven hundred years have flown.
Many a man of Edneved's kin
Hath stumbled in passion and fallen in sin!
Many a woman in sick despair
Had scorned, did she know it, the dead man's prayer;
Creeds and kingdoms have come and fled,
And faiths men died for, themselves are dead.

XLV.

But still, though envy, and lust, and greed
Have done their mischief, and won their meed,
Though avarice oft hath deformed the face,
And cankered the heart of the "kindly race,"
Though even the solid earth hath changed,
And the salt sea flows where the wild boar ranged,
The promise is not yet overthrown—
" In them that love Me shall mercy be shown."

XLVI.

And names both of high and of low degree
Trace from Edneved their pedigree;
All the Tudors—this to begin,
And Mostyn, and Mervyn, and Mytton, and Wynne,
And Puleston, and Penrhyn, and Pennant, and Pugh,
Cadwalader, Cayley, Cadogan, Cardew,
And Vaughans a many and Vaynols a few,
And all other Welshmen, betwixt me and you!

XLVII.

One is the vicar, where Edneved prayed;
  One on his hillside quarries the stone,
One is a neat little serving maid,
  One—is the Lady upon the Throne!
And one sails her ships on the Middleland sea,
  And one builds her bridges in Hindustan,
So health to them all, wheresoever they be,
  And peace to the soul of Edneved Vychan.

MORAL.

Now, children, for whom I have written this lay,
  The moral of it quite plain appears,
Write home once a week, say your prayers every day
  Keep your hair cut over your ears,
And if you want welcome, and supper, and fire,
  Spend your last sixpence in sending a wire.

I also append another version of the home return, which I have translated from the Welsh :—

THE HOME RETURN OF EDNEVED VYCHAN.

THE STORY AS GIVEN BY "CEIRIOG."

It is said that Edneved Vychan, among many others of that period, went to the Battle of the Holy Cross (the Crusades) leaving his wife and family at Llys Euryn until he returned victorious from the war.

But he remained so long from home, that many of his neighbours believed that he had been killed, and there was not a whisper to be heard nor an ankle nor bone of him to be had ever after. Among her neighbours, his wife began to despair, and when a certain gentleman proposed to marry her, the weak doubt that was on her mind became a great established fact, that nobody in his senses could disbelieve. The courtship went on fairly smoothly and the day of the wedding was fixed. There was a farm-house near to Llys Euryn, and one very wet night, there came some old beggar-man to ask for lodging and a morsel of food. He was tattered even more than a scarecrow, and as wet as a dunghill from top to toe. He ate and drank and went to the hayloft to rest for the night, sending his clothes back to the kitchen to be dried.

" Who can this old creature be?" said one of the chief retainers. " I have seen him better off years ago." " Perhaps so," said another, " it was not easy for you to see him or any other living man *worse* off." The large spinning wheel occupied much space that night in the farm-house kitchen, and the old wife of one of the workmen was spinning with it, until the house resounded from end to end. There came a stripling of a servant with the old beggarman's clothes to the fire, if clothes you can call two stockings, without feet, and an old " cinglet" with one arm to it. All that could be seen whole of the stockings was their tops, and it happened that those tops had been knitted with a "cross" on them all round. When the spinning wheel was silent, and the family were nodding by the fire, the old woman who had been spinning fell into a reverie.—" Those stockings she had knit with her own hands for Edneved Vychan before he started from home!" Edneved was in the hayloft, and next day his wife was to be married ! Among the harpers and minstrels we find the old Edneved singing and dancing. About eight o'clock the next night, the ceremony was over, and the banquet had begun in earnest and open house for all ! The strange minstrel said, "There used to be, when I was here before, an old harp." " It is in the loft above. That was my father's old harp," said his pallid young daughter, who was filling the strange harper's drinking horn. " Let me have it, and bring the key that belongs to it at once," said the old man. " No use," said the daughter, " there are not many tunes in it now."

But the old harp was brought, and the old rusty key, that was on its top, and it was not long before it was repaired,and the company were by this time in the height of their mirth and the married pair mingling in the dance.

The turn of the despised harp now came to give a start to the metre :— " By your leave," said the old stranger, " the people of the next farm have given me clothes to come to the marriage feast to-night, and if you will allow me to sing an old tune they have asked for, I will afterwards play the dance music." When the whole place was silent he played the piece " Ffarwel Edneved Fychan," and when he had reached the 10th stanza, the marriage feast was in a sense over. The wife was making for the door. Edneved raised his hand from the harp and exclaimed,

> Os bûm ar ffo—dro yn druan—gwallus
> I'm golli Gwenllian :
> Ni chollaf—ewch chwi allan—
> Na gwely—na thŷ—na thân."

He turned a second time to the dazed company,—after kissing his daughter—saying, "This was the last tune I wrote and composed before my departure from the Fatherland, this was the tune 'Farewell' to my dear Gwenllian. Hence let her go with her new husband,—my faithful harp! come *thou* to my arms." And after playing one other of his favourite airs he bade the company remain with him, to eat and drink and to rejoice that he who was dead had come to life again."

[It is possible that this story may be an historical fact. On referring to the time of Edneved Vychan, it will be seen that he lived in those troublous times, when many Britons went to the Crusades].

Edneved Vychan was an ancestor of Owain Tewdwr (Owen Tudor), who married Catherine, Queen Dowager of Henry V., and therefore an ancestor of our Most Gracious Queen Victoria, who is well known to take a warm interest in all Tudor Churches—of which Llandrillo is one, and which was redecorated and embellished with the Tudor Rose in 1897, in commemoration of the sixtieth year of her reign, at a cost of £60.

Queen Catherine was the eldest of the French Princesses, daughters of Charles VI. of France. Soon after the death of Henry V. (1422), his widow, Catherine, became enamoured of the manly graces of Owain Tewdwr. His introduction to her was singular. He, being a courtly and active gentleman, was commanded to dance before the Queen, and in a turn, not being able to recover himself, fell into her lap, as she sat on a little stool with many of her ladies about her. Queen Catherine, being a French-woman born, knew no difference between the English and Welsh nations, until her second marriage being published, Owain Tewdwr's kindred and countrymen were objected to—to disgrace him as most vile and barbarous, which made her desire to see some of his kinsmen,—whereupon Owain Tewdwr brought to her presence John ap Maredudd and Hywel ap* Llewelyn, his near cousins, and men

---

* AP. It is related that Rowland Lee, Bishop of Litchfield, and President of the Marches, in the reign of Henry VIII., sat on a Welsh cause, and, wearied with the quanity of Aps on the jury, directed that the panel should assume their last name, or that of their residence, and that Thomas ab Richard ap Hywel ap Ieuan Vychan should be reduced in future to the poor dissyllable Mostyn. In some copies of Gildas Gerontius, that the Cambro-British Kings used on the first coming of the Saxons, the appellation of Mac, instead of Mâb or Fâb, although now entirely used in Wales and preserved only in North Britain and Ireland. It has of late sank into the surname there, as Macpherson, Macdonald. So Ap, properly ab, from Mâb, the son, is generally lost in Wales, in the surnames. Bevan for Ap Evan, Powell for Ap Howell, Parry for Ap Harry. Ap is the banter of the English upon one pronunciation of Ab, the true abbreviation from Mâb, a son. (*Yorke's Royal Tribes of Wales.*)

of goodly stature and personage, but wholly destitute of bringing up and nurture ; for when the Queen had spoken to them in different languages, and they were not able to answer, she said they were the goodliest dumb creatures that ever she saw. (*Yorke's Royal Tribes of Wales.*)

In 1617, James 1st had progressed to Chester, and was attended by a great number of our countrymen, who came out of curiosity to see him. The weather was very dry, the roads dusty, and the King almost suffocated. He did not know well how to get civilly rid of them, when one of his attendants, putting his head out of the coach,said : "It was his Majesty's pleasure, that those, who were the best gentlemen, should ride forwards." Away scampered the Welsh, and one solitary man was left behind. " And so, sir," says the King to him, "and you are not a Gentleman, then ? " " Oh, yes, and please hur Majesty, hur is as good a Shentleman as the rest ; but hur Ceffyl, God help hur, is not so good.' Ceffyl (English—horse). *Cheval (French.)*

In the North aisle of the Parish Church, there is a tombstone bearing the inscription : " Underneath lyeth the body of Robert Conway of Pwllycrochan, Gentleman ; was buried here by leave of Robert Davies, Esq.,* 1693. This at once connects this Parish with Llannerch, St. Asaph, the owner of which (Sir Everard Cayley, Bart.), is also the owner of the lands surrounding the Parish Church. Llannerch came to the family on the marriage of Robert Davies,Gwysannau† (Flints.) with Anne, the eldest daughter and heiress of Sir Peter Mutton, Chief Justice of North Wales. Henry Wynn, Prothonotary of North Wales, sat for the County of Merioneth in the last Parliament of James the First,and died in 1671. This gentleman, writing to his father, Sir John, the Second of April, 1624, and speaking of Parliamentary business, says : " We sit very hard from seven in the morning until one in the afternoon, and after, from two of the clock in the afternoon until seven, in relation to Recusants, state of the Navy, motion against the Lord Treasurer, concerning stamps, used by him in stamping his name, which are left with his men. . These some held he might lawfully use, but kept safely by him, as the Keeper doth the Great Seal. I cannot chuse but remember what was said by Sir Peter Mutton of Llannerch, in the House, Sir Edward Coke sitting in the Chair : ' That this time, was not the first that stamps were used, for he had heard before he was born, that stamps were used here in this

* The old Public House, The Ship, generally known as "y Llan," was built by Robert Davies, Esq., 1736. It stood close to the Vicarage gate, with the large Hawthorn Tree resting on its roof; it was taken down in 1874, the new " Ship " having been erected by Whitehall Dod, Esq., 1873.

† Gwysanau, it is said, is a corruption of Hosanah, and allusory to the Alleluiatic victory over the Saxons and Picts beneath it.

Kingdom.' At which the whole House laughed : which is not to be forgotten in haste. To whom presently Sir Edward Coke called, ' Sir Peter Stamp.' "

In reference to Robert Davies, 'Esquire,' I may be allowed to explain the meaning of this title, which was the fourth class of Esquires, called white spurs. The ceremony was, that the King put about the recipient's neck a silver collar of Esses (SS), and conferred upon him a pair of silver spurs. The five ancient orders of Esquires were, first, those who are elect for the King's body : second, Knights' eldest sons : third, younger sons of the elder sons of Barons, and other nobles of higher estate : fourth, the white spurs by creation: and fifth, they who are so by office and by serving the Prince in any worshipful calling. This title of white spur was hereditary, and belonged only to the heir male of the family. (*Princes Worthies, Royal Tribes of Wales.*)

This gentleman, Robert Davies, who gave leave for the burial in this Church of *Robert Conway** of Pwllycrochan in 1693, was grandfather by his son, Robert Davies of Llannerch, an able Naturalist and Welsh Antiquary. He collected the valuable Library of MSS. that were at Llannerch. His grandson, Robert, the father of the last gentleman, was of a very hospitable turn : almost daily he had a led horse taken with him to St. Asaph, ready saddled, to bring home to Llannerch any friend that might not be so immediately ready to start with him. The old gardens at Llannerch were made by Mutton Davies in the foreign taste, with images and water tricks. Among the rest you were led to a sun-dial, which, as you approached, spouted in your face ; on it was written :—

> " Alas ! my friend, time soon will overtake you :
> And if you do not cry, by G—d I'll make you."

In reference to the connection of Robert Davies, Llannerch, with the Parish of Llandrillo, I have now to allude to a curious lawsuit that arose as to the " Afon Ganol," Latin " Medius Amnis," which divides the Counties of Denbigh and Carnarvon.

It appears that Queen Elizabeth being seized in fee of the Manor or Lordship of Denbigh and Denbighland in the fifth yeare of her Reigne graunts the said Lordship inter alia to Dudley Earle of

---

* An ancestor of this Robert Conway, Hugh Conway, by his Will in 1540, gave these directions:—" My body is to be buried or covered with earth beneath the Parish Church of Llandrillo. Also I leave five Pounds sterling to the aforesaid Church, to be disposed of in this manner, namely, fifty shillings of the same towards the building a certain approach or a porch at the door or entrance of the same Church : also the other aforesaid part of five Pounds for the construction of a chancel to the aforesaid Church." The Will is in Latin.

Leicester. The Earle of Leicester in the 21 Elizabeth graunts to Edward Conway and his heirs, one part of the Marsh called Morva Dinerth containing 34 acres of land, lyeing in Dinerth Township, between a certain stream dividing the Counties (Comitates) Denbigh and Caernarvon at the rent of £6 13s. 4d. It is presumed that this marsh was then in the nature of a common and the sea overflowed it at most spring tides in the yeare and soe Mr. Conway little minded it and soe the rent was not answerable to ye Queen nor to the Earle.

There is a channell on the West side of the marsh that divides the Counties of Denbigh and Caernarvonshire: at the lower end of which channell of water adjoining to the sea was as is reputed a creake wherein Boats and Shipps of 20 or 30 tun might at a certain time of flowing water gett in there and soe lye safe from storms, and soe it hath ever continued from beyond memory till 1687. Mr. Conway legally conveyed this marsh to the ancestors of Robert Davies, Esq., and neither he nor his ancestors did not much mind the marsh but his Tenants' cattle grazed there sometimes.

A Mr. Pugh (Penrhyn) was owner of another marsh that runs along southerly from the sea on the West side of the channell lying in Caernarvonshire had under some pretence gott some small rent of the marsh in Dinerth in Denbighshire, for many yeares (perhaps beyond memory) and in 1687 built a bridge upon the creake and stopped the sea from overflowing and also all boates and small vessells from getting in there for shelter in stormy weather.

Mr. Davies in 1688 got possession and received proffitts of the marsh in Dinerth. But Mr. Davies brought his ejectment in Caernarvonshire, and by Tricking got possession in April 1693, but it was after a Triall and noe Defence made by Mr. Davies, because he had been advised that the Judges of Caernarvon could not try the cause for lands lyeing in Denbighshire. Counsel advised that it would be proper for Mr. Davies to sue the Deputy Sheriffe for delivering possession out of his proper County, and also as to what course the landowners should take against Mr. Pugh to remove the Bridge and whether it ought not to be taken down that boats and small shipps may have usual shelter as time out of mind it hath been used as a Creake or Harbour. The lawsuit appears to have resulted in the disputed territory continuing in the possession of Mr. Pugh.

In the early part of the 17th Century a Mr. Hugh Stodart, of Deganwey wrote to begge the favour of Mr. Mutton Davies and his son to grant him the libertie to sett nettes upon Llansantffraide sandes to which request the following was the answer : —

Sir, My son and I thank you for your kind present (fish) and we are both willing to promote the fishing trade in the hands of soe good a friend, and therefore you are at liberty to sell your netts for this season in such places as our interest lies, provided you own our right and express as much to the tenants that live next ye place. I presume if you have successe you will sometimes send us a taste of ye fish you take in ye meantime, I will tye you to no other condition who am,

Your loveing friend to
serve you
M. D.

(Unpublished MSS.)

I now pass on to a very interesting feature in this Parish, viz., the ancient Fishing Weir or Wear. There was formerly a Monastery at Conway ; it was founded by the Second Llewelyn, Prince of North Wales, in 1198. The Monks were Cistercian. These Monks required a supply of fish. This old Weir without doubt was part of the property of these Monks, for the name of it in Welsh is to the present day Rhos Fynach — Rhos Monachorum, or the Feu Farm of the Monks. It is possible, from the fact of fish being so important to the Monks, that we sometimes find a fish an emblem of our Saviour. The Greek for a fish is ἰχθὺς and if we take these letters separately, they will make (in Greek) the following sentence :—" Jesus Christ, the Son of God, the Saviour."

But it is not to be forgotten that—

The emblem of the crossed fishes on a tomb is indicative of its having been that of a Christian, and has its origin earlier than the necessity of Fish to Monks, and has relation to the miraculous draught of fishes and to Christ feeding the multitude from five small loaves and two small fishes. The emblem or sign was in use at the time of the first persecutions, even under Nero 64—68, and certainly in Diocletian's time 303—313. The emblem was Two Fishes crossed.

Vide Mrs. Jamison's Early Christian Art, and the legend was plural, viz., Ἰχθύες (Fishes). It was the secret sign of Christianity as the Cross was the outward symbol of Christ.

The Weir is also called in Welsh " Gored Wyddno."

It is held under a Charter, a very ancient parchment, written in Monkish Latin, and is signed " Leycester." The date of this document is the 17th year of the Reign of Queen Elizabeth, viz., 1575, and is now in the possesion of Mr. William Horton, Bryndinarth, the owner of the Rhos Fynach Estate. The name of the Farm to which the Weir is attached, would seem to prove that the Weir is of much greater antiquity than that grant, having been erected by the Monks during the period they were settled at Conway from 1198 to 1289, which would make the Weir to be about 650 years old. In 1289, Edward I., having conquered Wales and not wishing to have so powerful a body of Welsh clergy in his new town of Conway, removed the Abbey "abbatia Aberconweusis" to Maenan, near Llanrwst, ten miles from Conway, with the consent of the Pope. He at the same time took from the Monks all their possessions in Conway, giving them in lieu thereof others of equal or greater value near Maenan.

The present Vicarage was built in 1762. The following is the inscription on a tombstone in Llandrillo Churchyard:—

"To the memory of Isaac Charles, Clerk, late Vicar of this Parish, buried July ye 9, 1763. He was a worthy Clergyman and General Benefactor to this Church in building in 1762 a Decent House for the Vicarage thereof which he lived to finish but not to enjoy."*

The Vicarage was enlarged by me in 1869, by the addition of the present Dining Room and Bedroom above, and the building of bow windows to all the rooms in the front of the Vicarage: also an underground water tank, containing about 3,500 gallons rain water, since superseded by the introduction of town's water in 1893. The Church and Vicarage were first lighted with gas in 1887.

PWLLYCROCHAN.

Everyone has by this time heard of Pwllycrochan. But everyone is not acquainted with the history of the House, which was the quaint, old-fashioned, brick family mansion of the Hollands and Williamses.

Sir David Erskine, wishing for a larger residence, metamorphosed the house, into a very square solid-looking block, which his widow (Lady Silence Erskine), the only child of the Rev. Hugh Williams, of Plas Isaf, Conway, beautified into a lofty Elizabethan edifice, wherein all traces of each preceding stage were obliterated. It is now (1898) a most stately mansion, perfectly situated in the midst of lovely woods.

There are various meanings given of the—to some—unpronounceable word Pwllycrochan.

---

*The Parish Terrier, exhibited in ye year 1791, contains the following entry:—"The Mansion was built about 30 years ago and ye present Vicar (the Rev. Evan Ellis) in ye year 1777 took down that part of ye old Building wh. was left standing when ye new House was erected and has rebuilt on a larger scale and with different materials. The present Building consists of a Passage wh. communicates wth ye Kitchen on ye right hand, and on ye left are a Scullery, Cellar, Store-room, Pantry, and over all is a large Room six yards by five. This Building is mostly built of Bricks and covered with slates and ye whole is cieled."

Pwllycrochan—Pwllyrochain—hole of moaning, indicating that there had been great slaughter in the immediate neighbourhood. On a tombstone, in the Church, 1693, it is spelt Pwllycrochan. Sir Thomas Erskine, Cambo House, Fifeshire, wrote to me, giving his explanation as that of

> Pwllycrochon—the Hollow in the great Ash—"onn."
> Thus—" Llwyn onn — Ash Grove."

The Four Cross Road above Pwllycrochan, boasted formerly of an Inn, of great notoriety—very appropriately named "The Four Crosses" (briefly " Y ffôr "—the Road), and kept by a respectable old dame, Dolly Evans. Here it was that " Militia and Volunteer Meetings and Wakes were held ; here rents were received, and tithes were set to the highest bidder ; here justice business was transacted ; and here it was beyond all doubt, that when a large party were 'at high tea' on the ground floor, the dancers upstairs plied 'the light fantastic toe' so *heavily*, that the whole of the ceiling, unable to endure such perverse levity, yielding the preference to the legitimate force of gravity, came down bodily in a few huge slabs, and buried tea-makers and tea-drinkers—pots and all—cream and sugar and all—butter and eggs and all—without respect of persons or things—men or measures—women or best caps—in one undistinguishable ruination of smashed crockery—bent pewter—spilt milk—crushed ribbons—broken heads—'Tea, Coffee and Hot Water on the shortest notice.' "

The Road at the back of Pwllycrochan, and passing the Four Crosses Inn, was formerly the route of the Holyhead Mail. This antiquated vehicle, in commencing the descent to Mochdre from Gallt y Cribau, toppled over to the right and trotted down the hill, past Tan'rallt, without injury to man or beast, for whom entertainment was duly provided at "The Eagles" hard by, instead of their carcases becoming, as well they might, a prey to all birds and dogs.

It may surprise still more, people of the present day, to hear that the line was continued across Conwy Ferry, behind Penmaen Bach, down to the romantic Pass of Sychnant, and then over Penmaen Mawr, by a route now difficult to trace or even believe.

The first entries in the Parish Register are as follow :—

> Birth—April 9th, 1693.
> Funeral—July 2nd, 1693.
> Marriage—August 9th, 1693.

The Sun-dial was the gift of Mary Jarvis, of Dinerth, in 1755. On the base of the column, is the date 1712. This probably served as the column of a former sun-dial. Under the bevelled edge - "Th. Owen, 1756."

There are five townships in the Parish of Llandrillo-yn-rhos --Dinerth, Rhiw, Mochdre, Llwydcoed, Cilgwyn, Colwyn and Eirias (Ayros in time of Edward I). Eirias is an independent Township, maintaining its own poor and making separate rates, having its own overseers for the purpose.

A detached portion of the Township was a narrow strip of land, including Glanymor, Rhos, as far as Rhyd Farm, formerly known as Rhyd y Cerrig Gwynion (The Ford of the White Stones.)

CURIOUS ENTRIES IN THE VESTRY BOOKS.

1770-1 Church Mize* at the rate of 4d. per hd.

1772 Pd Elizabeth Hughes to buy an ass 0 10 9

1774 4th Day of April. The Inhabitants of the Parish of Llandrillo-yn-Rhos agreed with John Thomas for the sum of Seven Pounds seven shillings for teaching all the Parishioners that has a mind to learn to sing Psalms from this time to All Saints every Saturday Eve and Sundays.

Evan Ellis, Vicar.

1774			
For Rushes in the Church	0	9	0
Ale for the singers	0	10	0
Candles	0	4	0
Thomas Davies, for writing all the Parish business	1	1	0
John Thomas, Singing Master	3	13	6

1774 For killing a wood cat 0 3 6

1775 Lost in a Guinea short of weight 0 1 6

1777 Paid for the shroud of Hannah Parry, 2/7 .... 0 2 7
   ,, for the New Stocks at Groes 1 0 0

1777 24th April Perused and allowed (having been first signed and verified on oath) before me, one of His Majesty's Justices of the Peace for the said County Denbigh. Jno. Jones.

---

* Mise. The term mise or mize is not Saxon but old French, S and Z being interchangeable letters; it was often written " Mize." It comes from the Latin "mittere," which was written "mettre" in the Middle Ages. The change of "i" into "e" took place in very early times in low Latin, e.g., "magester" for "Magister." The term mise was used in law of money given by way of compensation or agreement to purchase any liberty, vide. "The mise of Lewis in the reign of Henry III." (1216—1272). Mise in Law also, came to be written "Mease" for "Messuage." It was also a word used to designate a tax or tollage. In Wales, the term was technically applied to the gift of £5,000 paid to every new Prince on his entry to the Principality. It was also a tribute paid in the County Palatine of Chester at the change of the owner of the Earldom - anciently given in cattle, corn, or wine, in both cases.

1777   To Pay Owen Roberts of Bryn y Cariweh the sum of one Pound per yr

1777   6 lb: Candles at Crismas Morning .... o 4 o
New door for the pin fould   ...   .o 7 6
4 yards of Ribonds for the Singers .... o 3 o

Do. /78 for instructing the Singers every Sunday morning and evening before
Prayers as long as he continues in the Parish of Llandrillo and Doeth
his Duty.

1780   Feb. 20. A Vestry held in the Parish Church of Llandrillo Publick
Notice being Given the Sunday Before it was Ordered and agreed on
By the Minister And the Inhabitance of the aforesd Parish to Pay to any
Person for fox killing in the aforesd Parish two shillings and six pence
And One Shilling and three pence for a Puppy

May 31st   At a Vestry then held and Lawfully called in the Parish Church of
1784   Llandrillo in Rhos. It was agreed and allowed by the Minister and
the Inhabitants then present that William Hughes of Llwydcoed in the
same Parish aforesd a Liberty of erecting a new Pew or seat, and the
breadth of the seat is to be three Foot and a Half and the place where
she is to be build is on the South Isle of the afores Church Between
the Pulpit and the Large Door.
allowed by us as wittness our hands Richard Jackson Curate.
Inhabitants, etc.

April 29, 1787. A Vestry was held on Sunday Evining at Hugh Hughes
Glanmor, Parish Clerk of Llandrillo in Rhos to settle the overseers for
gathir tax six Pence in Pound.

16th   That David Thomas a Parochial child is to be Bound an Apprentice
day of to Hugh Hughes of Mochdre to learn the art and mystery of shoemaking
June   for the term of seven years and likewise he is to be Vituald by Robert Jones
1787   of Tygwyn for the term of two years of the abovemention in consideration of Three Pounds and three shillings.

April 12   David Thomas a Parochial child be bound an Apprentice to Evan Jones
1788   of Garthbach in the Parish of Llangwstenin in the County of Carnarvon to be Victuald for 2 years term and that Evan Jones is to cloath
him for the term of seven years and likewise is to give him Meat and
Drink for the remainder term of five years.

April 12   Rachel Parry a Parochial Child is to be Cloathed and Nourish'd
1788   hereafter by Hugh Hughes of Mochdre in consideration of the sum of
Six Pounds six shillings for the term of three years to be paid him
yearly Two Pounds two shillings and the sd Child must work as much
as will be reasonably required and must not be indulg'd by any of the
Inhabitants to prevent her to be brought on in an Industrious way and
the sd Hugh Hughes is hereby bound to behave himself in a fair and
Honest manner towards the said Child

Nov. 1st   Did Allowd to Grace Thomas of Eirias two 'Barrels of Coals and a
1790   spining wheel, and so forth. Did Allowed to Anne the wife of John
Thomas ' Bryntirion ' two " Barrels of Coals.

Nov. 1
1790   two Barrels of Coals and a Spining Wheel

yͤ 9ᵗʰ of April 1790	Agreed that the Votation of yͤ tythe is settled upon the Rector (Bish of St. Asaph) of Llandrillo and other materials both Mills, Tythes Wears, Coals, Mines and other Minerals.

Tythes	Reated
18 . 10 . 0	Dinerth Corn
2 . 0 . 0	Dinerth Heay
8 . 10 . 0	Mochdre Corn
8 . 0 . 0	Llwydcoed Dᵒ·
4 . 0 . 0	Killgwyn Dᵒ·
10 . 0 . 0	Eirias Dᵒ·

41 . 0 . 0   To be collected as another inhabitants and land holders

1791   David Hughes Rhosfynach for maintaining from hence the clothing of Robert the son of Jane Thomas of Aberhod and to learn the art of Husbandry for five Pounds 10/ for the space of five years.

June 8ᵗʰ 1793   It was further allowᵈ to John Williams overseer to discharge John Roberts Militiaman · for the township of Dinerth in the County of Denbigh and to hire a man in the stade of him the said John Williams is to hire a man with his own money and the Parish Liable to remit him the same sum

April 19ᵗʰ 1793   It was furtherᵈ agree to get a Law Book for the use of the Parish.

Nov. 30ᵗʰ 1793   It is further orderᵈ that Mᵣ· Jno. Oldfield of tne Furnace be appointed the Solicitor to act for and On Behalf of our Parish whom we Direct the Parish Officer for the time being to consult upon every necesary Occasion and for his trouble in that respect we Engage to allow him an Anual salary of One Guinea and also engage to pay him the further sum of one Guinea for every Pauper or One Family that may be absolutely removed from our Parish by and under his the sᵈ Jno. Oldfield advice and the like sum for every Apeal that may hapen to be projected by our Parish Officers for the time being wherin we should be successful.

May 2ⁿᵈ 1795   At the same Vestry it was orderᵈ to Feby —— shift Beatgown and Pretty coat

June 24ᵗʰ 1797   We the said Parishioners do agree that John Evans is to have NO more money For playing the Basoon.

April 6ᵗʰ 1799   Allowᵈ to Robᵗ Thomas Smith Mochdre Half x tun of Coals.

March 4 1801   Allowᵈ William Thomas of Dinerth Issa One Pound One Shilling per year for playing the Basoon Beginning the 6 of Fpiphany

1804   Vestry held at the " Four Crosses "* 9 Day of March

1818   Sinking ground on South Side of the Church 1 0 0

1819   Ordered that three Prayer Books published by Gee and respectably bound be purchased, two for the Churchwardens and one for the use of the Clerk.

* The last Vestry at " Four Crosses " appears to have been held April 19th, 1821.

1821   24th Day of October.   General Vestry held in Llandrillo Church.
Thos. Alban, Vicar.

(There appear to have been also Select Vestries, whose proceedings,
Resolutions and Transactions were examined at a General Vestry.)

April 17   There is an entry : " By paid for ale allowed and drank at Select
1827   Vestries last year being ignorant of the Magistrates Directions for not
paying for ale at the Vestries   £3 . 18 . 5½ "
Thos. Alban, Vicar.

	£	s.	d.
1828. 30 D of April			
Pd: Robert Jones for printing 100 Handbills (Sacrilege) ...	0	7	6
Expenses of Journey to Liverpool respecting Sacrilege......	2	8	0
Time and trouble 4 days	0	12	0
2 Journeys to Conway on Do.	0	4	0
Paid Reward officers for discovering the person guilty of the Sacrilege	10	0	0
Ordered that the step of the Dial be properly repaired and that the Church be whitewashed			
Pd: Wm Hughes steps to Dial	4	0	0
Car: of stones to Do.	0	7	6
Mason ½ day at Do.	0	1	3

1830   Steps to Dial   0 . 4 . 0
Carriage of stones 2 Mason 1/3 ½ Day   0 . 8 . 9
Foxes killed and paid for
From 1818 to 1833
68 Foxes   £ 10 . 7 . 0

19th Day of September 1833
It was agreed and ordered that an English 4to Bible and an
English Prayer Book be immediately procured for the use
of the Church

1835	Thos. Foulkes, Groes, for candles, Bellrope & mould Candles	0	14	3
	16 lbs. Bolt Iron for the Bell at 5d per lb.	0	6	8
	Journey to put the Bolt thro' the Frame...	0	3	0

30th Day of June 1836				
Stone Posts for the Church Yard Gate	2	0	0
Cartage	0	15	0
Iron gates 400 lbs. at 3½ per lb.............................	5	16	8
2 Men for three day's work in setting the gates	0	18	0
Boring Holes in the Posts	0	1	6
One Day's Team	0	7	0

18th May 1838 an adjourned Vestry was held at the Vicarage House

June 25, 1840 A Vestry was held in Llandrillo Public House and
adjourned thence to the Vicarage House

May 18th 1843 Vestry held in Llandrillo Church and thence adjourned to the Ship Public House.

2nd Day of June 1847
Vestry held Ship Tavern Llandrillo

1856	New Bier	0	14	0

At a Vestry held this 31 Day of August 1827 in Llandrillo Church, persuant to legal Notice, it was ordered and agreed that in Lieu and stead of the Church Loan of Six Pence in the Pound ordered and agreed to be laid and levied at the Vestry held the 26th April 1827 but not yet levied or collected, that a Church Loan of One Shilling in the Pound be laid and levied for the Service of the current year.

Ordered also that the Premium of Ten Pounds agreed to be paid to the Person who should discover, or give such Information as might lead to the Discovery of the Person who sacriligiously robbed this Church of the Communion Plate, be paid by the Church Wardens to John Rowlands, Pawnbroker, Liverpool;—who it appears detected Hugh Williams with Part of the Plate in his possession ; and for which the said Hugh Williams was tried, found guilty, and ordered to be transported for Seven Years.

It appearing that Mr. John Miller, Police Officer, Liverpool, had been extremely active and industrious in conducting the Prosecution of the said Hugh Williams and in saving harmless this Parish from all the attendant Law Expenses, which he promises shall be paid by the County of Lancaster ; this Vestry taking into Consideration his Services and kind Assistance, request his acceptance of Ten Pounds as a Mark of their approbation of his Conduct in this Business which said Sum of Ten Pounds they order and direct the Church Wardens to pay him accordingly and the same shall be allowed in their account.

It is agreed to accept from the Vicar, for the Communion Service, of two plated Cups and a Plate or Paten ; upon each of which the words "Llandrillo yn Rhos" are engraved.

Thos. Alban, Vicar.   John Poyser.
D. Erskine.   David Jones.

Richd. Butler Clough.
John Jones.   } Church
Samuel Bartley.   } Wardens.

1823 That a Bill due to Messrs. Poole and Harding amounting to Three Pounds and 8d. for repairing and car: of Bassoon for Reeds for do. and for Hautboy Box and Postage   ... 3 0 8

1827 That the Thanks of the Vestry be given to Reverend Thomas Alban, Vicar of this Parish for his handsome present of two plated Cups and a plate or Paten upon each of which the words "Llandrillo-yn-Rhos" are engraved.

D. Erskine.
Richd. Butler Clough.

TOMBSTONES.

In Ch. Yd. now, used to be in the centre of the Church. "Here lyeth the body of Margaret Vaughan, widow, wife to Henry Vaughan of Glyn, and daughter to Bonam Norton of Straton in ye Co: of Salop Esqre who departed this life ye 8th day of Decr. and was buried ye 19th in the 92nd year of her age Anno 1699.

THE BELL

bears date 1752, and was cast by Ralph Ashton, Wigan.

EDWARD HUGHES, } Churchwardens.
WILLIAM EVANS,

JOHN GWYNN being Vicar.

SINECURE RECTORS.

10 Aug.,

1302   "Hugh *Lyversedge*, Clerk, admitted to Llandrillo." Lambeth Registers.

1558   Ellis Price, L.L.D.

1660   James Cresset was of Upton Cresset and Counde, Salop.

1558   Elis ap Richard had a dispensation to hold the Rectory of Llanddoget (near Llanrwst) with this Vicarage.

1610   Griffith Prichard, A.M., Rector of Llangelynin (dioc. Bangor) 1613, Canon of Bangor 1626, Rector of Llangynhafal (near Ruthin) 1626, Will proved 9 May 1633.

1695   John Stodart, A.B. (Jes. Coll. Ox.), Master of Wrexham School 1691.

1718   Thomas Lloyd, A.M.

HUGH CONWAY'S WILL.

1540   " My body is to be buried or covered with earth beneath the parish Church of Llandrillo. Also, I leave five Pounds sterling to the aforesaid Church, to be disposed of in this manner, namely, fifty shillings of the same,. towards building or making a certain approach or one porch for the entrance of the same Church; also, the other aforesaid part of the five pounds, towards the building of a chancel to the aforesaid Church."—*Archæologia Cambrensis*, 1880.

DOMESTIC STATISTICS.

Amongst other parochial documents is one containing the following domestic statistics for the year 1831 of the Parish of Llandrillo-yn-Rhos, considered, for the most part, in two portions, namely, the Denbighshire portion, and the Carnarvonshire portion (Eirias), and signed by the then Vicar (Rev. Thomas Alban) :—

Inhabited houses : Denbighshire portion, 184 ; Eirias, 50.

Number of families occupying same : Denbighshire, 185 ; Eirias, 48.

Houses now building : Denbighshire, 2 ; Eirias, 0.

Other houses uninhabited : Denbighshire, 4 ; Eirias, 2.

Families chiefly in agriculture : Denbighshire, 37 ; Eirias, 12.

Families in trade, manufactures : Denbighshire, 33 ; Eirias, 4.

All other families not comprised in the preceding: Denbighshire, 114; Eirias, 32.

Number of persons, including children, of whatever age : Denbighshire, 871 (426 males, 445 females); Eirias, 262 (132 males, 130 females).

Total number of males twenty years old : Denbighshire, 222 ; Eirias, 50.

Males employed in agriculture, occupiers of land employing labourers : Denbighshire, 48 ; Eirias, 7.

Occupiers of land not employing labourers : Denbighshire, 13 ; Eirias, 5.

Labourers employed in agriculture : Denbighshire, 112 ; Eirias, 18.

Males employed in manufactory or any machinery : Denbighshire, 41 ; Eirias, 2.

Males employed in retail trades, etc.: Denbighshire, 3 ; Eirias, 0.

Wholesale merchants, bar keepers, and professions : Denbighshire, 5 ; Eirias, 1.

Labourers in preceding classes or husbandry : Denbighshire, 3 ; Eirias, 23.

Cotter males twenty-one years old, disabled or retired : Denbighshire, 1 ; Eirias, o.

Servants : Total, 273 ; males under twenty, 1 ; ditto above twenty, 1 ; female servants, 54.

Persons in 1831, 871 ; ditto in 1821, 760 ; increase, 111—" no particulars of such increase.—Thos. Alban."

The following are a few details as to the population, etc., in 1821 :—Inhabited houses : Denbighshire, 82 ; Eirias, 40.   Families occupying : Denbighshire, 93 ; Eirias, 42.   Houses uninhabited : Denbighshire, 2 ; Eirias, 3.   Families chiefly employed in agriculture : Denbighshire, 62 ; Eirias, 32.   Families employd in trade, manufactures, and handicrafts : Denbighshire, 14 ; Eirias, 4. All other families not comprised in the two preceding classes : Denbighshire, 16 ; Eirias, 6.   Persons : Denbighshire, 760 (369 males, 391 females) ; Eirias, 200 (104 males, 96 females).

THE CHURCHWARDEN'S BOOK

contains the following interesting records :—

In 1818, a Church Rate of 6d. in the £, £45 11s. od.—Thos. Alban, Vicar.

Baptisms : 1811, 19 ; 1812, 21 ; 1813, 24 ; 1814, 17 ; 1815, 27 ; 1816, 13 ; 1817, 19 ; 1818, 15 ; 1819, 24 ; 1820, 26.

Burials : 1811, 15 ; 1812, 15 ; 1813, 14 ; 1814, 12 ; 1815, 12 ; 1816, 16 ; 1817, 10 ; 1818, 18 ; 1819, 9 ; 1820, 6.

Marriages : 1811, 4 ; 1812, 9 ; 1813, 14 ; 1814, 5 ; 1815, 3 ; 1816, 9 ; 1817, 14 ; 1818, 11 ; 1819, 13 ; 1820, 6.

Total number of unentered Baptisms, 44, viz.:—at Colwyn Chapel, 12 ; Mochtre do., 32.   Do. of Funerals, Colwyn Chapel, 5.—Thos. Alban, Vicar.

Kind reader, pray forgive me for giving here a short but to me interesting record of my own work in this Parish and neighbourhood.   First, Parochial.*

	£	s.	d.
School Cottage built in 1869 (since demolished, site of Tan-y-Bryn)	200	0	0
Sunday afternoon Service commenced June 18th, 1871, discontinued September 17th, 1871, in a Carpenter's shed, kindly lent by a Nonconformist (the late Mr. Abel Roberts).			
In 1872, Mission Room built	200	0	0
Parish Church, Organ by Hill & Son	215	0	0
Organ Chamber, 1875	150	0	0

* When I first joined the Board of Guardians at Conway, in 1869, the Railway Company were assessed at £125 a mile for 16 miles.   I was the means of getting the Company raised by degrees to the present figure, viz.: £1800 per mile.   The Railway Company are assessed within the Union at £26.000 ; the total assessment of the Union is £194,000.   In 1879, I took an active part in having Llandrillo-yn-Rhos removed from the Petty Sessional Division of Llanrwst to that of Abergele, and I have now succeeded in having Colwyn Bay constituted a separate Petty Sessional Division ; this was decided at the Quarter Sessions held at Denbigh, on April 9th, 1898.

Organ enlarged, 1875	50	0	0
Wall on South and West side of Church Yard and new Hearse House built by Mrs. Frost, Minydon, 1877 ...	100	0	0
Stained Glass S.E. Window —" The Resurrection," 1872 ...	75	0	0
East Window—" The Crucifixion "	400	0	0
N.E. Window —" Visit of the Magi "	80	0	0
S. Window, 1892, by Mrs. Radcliffe —"Ascension"	100	0	0

1877	The Church painted and Pews washed and revarnished, also Dossal	50	0	0
1879	Brass Altar Desk, given by Miss Williams, Fron Haul, Mold	5	0	0
1879	Velvet Altar Cloth (Public Subscription)...	30	0	0
	Alms-Dish by Garden-Box Contributions	5	5	0
	Bible, Prayer Book, 2 Altar Books and Office Books ...	5	5	0
1884	Church re-roofed	500	0	0
1888	St. Paul's consecrated, cost	7000	0	0
1896	Organ enlarged by Conacher	300	0	0
	Water Engine, & Pipe-laying...............	50	0	0
1897	Jubilee Decoration	60	0	0
	Gas Fittings (Incandescent)	10	0	0

COLWYN.

Extracted from a History of the Diocese of St. Asaph, by Rev. D. R. Thomas, Archdeacon and Canon of St. Asaph :—

This district, originally assigned in 1844, and re-arranged in 1872, consists of the townships of Colwyn, Eirias, and a portion of Cilgwyn out of Llandrillo, a portion of Llanelian, and the hamlet of Graig out of the parish of Llysfaen ; with a population of 900.

The Ecclesiastical Commissioners have also assigned to it (1872), out of the rectorial tithes of Llandrillo, a tithe-rentcharge of £395 17s. 3d., in lieu of their previous payments (e.g., a tithe-rentcharge of £74, granted in April, 1844 ; and a second, of £37 6s. 5d., in 1855). A glebe house (towards this a sum of £500 previously granted, to augment the living, by Queen Anne's Bounty ; and two sums of £200 each to meet similar benefactions, have been applied) has also been built this year on a site given by Mr. Abraham Whittaker, late of Minydon. It is in the gift of the Vicar of Llandrillo.

The Church of St. Catherine was built in 1837 as a chapel-of-ease to Llandrillo, and so continued till gazetted with a district of its own in 1844. It was erected through the instrumentality of Richard Butler Clough, of Minydon (ob. 1844), to whose widow, Catherine, the Church is dedicated.

PERPETUAL CURATES AND VICARS.

1844 Hughes, Thomas, Lampeter, V. Llandrillo, 1855.
1855 Lewis, Evan, B.D., Lampeter, V. Llanfair Talhaiarn, 1866.
1866 Jones, John David, Lampeter.
1888 Price Jones, David, B.A., Lampeter.
1893 Griffiths, John, A.M. Oxon.

LLANGWSTENYN.

I am indebted for the following accounts of the Parishes of Llangwstenin, &c., to the "History of the Diocese of St. Asaph," by the Rev. D. R. Thomas, M.A. Oxon., Canon and Archdeacon of St. Asaph :—

In the " *Taxatio* " of Pope Nicholas, 1291, " Llangustenin " is described as a Capella of Abergele, and therewith annexed to the Prebend of the Archdeacon. To the same effect it is returned in the valor as appropriate to the Archdeaconry, and its value given as £6 13s. 4d.

The Church, dedicated to Cystenyn Fendigaid, Pendragon of the Britons and father of Digain the founder of Llangernyw, was rebuilt in 1843, at a cost of £780. It consists of a single aisle, with a western gallery and bell turret. The east window of five lights contains a few remains of the old stained glass, thus described in the *Cambro-Briton* : —" Here are some fragments of elegantly painted glass. The first figure is our Saviour, the second St. George and the Dragon, the third, Justice with her balance, in the one end of which is represented a sinner, and in the other his sins, and the devil underneath pulling down the latter to make it preponderate. In the south window of the chancel, are the following—in the centre, Sanctus Petrus with his keys, on his right Nicholaus, and on his left St. Catharina, and underneath ' Orate pro animabus,'" etc.

INCUMBENTS.

1683 Owen, Humphrey.	1763 Owen, Owen.
1745 Williams, William.	1766 Edwards, Edward
1749 Lloyd, David, B.A.	1783 Pugh, Richard.
1755 Ellis, Zaccheus.	1831 Hughes, J. E.
1757 Bennett, Gilbert	1846 Roberts, Edward, A.M.
1887 Davies, William.	

LLYSFAEN.

Originally it seems to have formed a portion of Llandrillo, as evidenced by certain mutual obligations laid down in the old terriers, and confirmed by the Commutation Returns. The " *Taxatio* " of 1291 simply notes, " *Rectoria di Lisnaen* taxatur £4, non decimat"; and the "*Valor Eccles.*" of Henry VIII. only states its clear value to be £12 0s. 4d., on which £1 4s. 0½d. were payable to the King as tenths; but the terriers record that whilst on the one hand " half the township of Penmaen tithes to the Rector of Llandrillo, and out of the other moiety the Vicar of Llandrillo has a third part, paying twenty shillings for four sermons; and the tithes of one day's math in Gweirglodd " *Isallt* " doth belong unto the township of Meynan (in Llanelian), or the sum of one shilling in lieu of the same; whereof six-pence belongs to the Rector of Llandrillo, four pence to the Rector of Llanelian, and two pence to the Vicar of Llandrillo."

LLANELIAN.

The original name of this place appears to have been that which is still retained for its chief township, Bodleuyn; but it has been superseded for the parish by the one derived from its proximity to the notorious " Cursing Well," Ffynnon Elian. " The ceremony (of cursing) is performed by the applicant standing upon a certain spot near the well, whilst the owner of it reads a few passages of the Sacred Scriptures, and then, taking a small quantity of water, gives it to the former to drink, and throws the residue over his head, which is repeated three times, the party continuing to mutter his imprecations in whatever terms his vengeance may dictate." (*Lewis's Topographical Dictionary*). At that time (1832), it was visited by hundreds of persons for that villanous purpose. It has been stated that a man lost £80 rather than ask for it back again, for fear of being put into the well, and that "a person in England pined away under the belief that she had been so cursed," in the township of Eirias, which is ecclesiastically in the parish of Llandrillo, but for civil purposes has its own independent guardians and overseers. The terrier of 1730 throws much light on the relation of this parish as well to that of Llysfaen as to that of Llandrillo, which is, no doubt, the Mother Church of both. "But there are four sermons due from the sayd rector and vicar to the parish of Llanelian, there to be preached by the sayd vicar on four severall Sundays in the year, or the summe of twenty shillings per ann. to be paid by the sayd rector or vicar to the rector of Llanelian in lieu of the s'd sermons."

EGLWYSRHOS.

Eglwys Rhos, otherwise Llanrhos, more fully "Llanfair yn Rhos," *i.e.*, "St. Mary's in Rhos," indicates the influence of the Cistercian Monks of Aberconwy. In the Churchyard a tombstone to the memory of "Robertus Pue de Penrhyn ob: 1659" bears the hexameter—

> Nosta sub hoc sculpto pars est vilissima saxo
> Meus sua fert coelum jure, cadaver humen.

Anglice—

> Our basest part is under this carved stone,
> Its soul hath heaven by right ; earth, flesh and bone.

At Penrhyn there was a Free Chapel* endowed by a grant of Pope Nicholas with three-fourths of the tithe of the township, and mentioned in the valor of 1535 as "Libera Capella Beatæ Mariæ de Penryn valet clare 20/- inde proxima parte regi 2/-." The family continued to profess the Roman Catholic faith and to support a priest as domestic chaplain for a long period after the Reformation. —*Archdeacon Thomas's History of the Diocese of St. Asaph.*

In Wynne's History of Wales the lineage of the various Kings and Princes of Wales and the Kings of England is traced up to Brutus, who it is stated first inherited this Island and called it

---

* " Free Chapel of the Blessed Mary of Penryn."

Britain. And therefore we find that the Welsh, the ancient proprietors of Britain, called themselves Gomeri or Cymry, and their language Cymraeg, which words bear so great analogy to the original appellation whence they are derived, that we may reasonably conclude the true ancient Britons or Welsh (the Celts or Gauls) to be the genuine descendents of Gomer, the eldest son of Japhet, who was the eldest son of Noah, and they migrated from the Provinces of Upper Asia, to the north side of the Euxine Sea, and, as they were called Cimmerians in Asia, they communicated their name to that famous Strait which has since been called Cimbrian or Cimmerian Bosphorus. The affinity between the Celts or Gauls and the ancient Britons, is further counted with respect to religion, language, laws and customs.—*Owen's History*.

MISCELLANEA.

M.S.—Owen (Tudor) was son of Meredith ap Tudor ap Gronow ap Edneved or Edneved Vychan, Baron of Brinffanigle in Denbighland, Lord of Cricketh, Chief Justice and Chief Councillor to Llewelyn ap Iorwerth, Prince of all Wales.

M.S.—The Island (Priestholme, commonly known as Puffin Island) is in the County of Flint, to which it is supposed it was once joined by an arm of land running past the Ormesheads, from the neighbourhood of Rhyl.

PROF. RHYS ON PLACE NAMES.

Professor Rhys, Oxford, in his Presidential Address, at the Llandudno Eisteddfod, July, 1896,

Dealing with the Etymology of local place names, said that Llandudno was called after a saint named Tudno, whose history was almost wholly lost. He, however, took it for granted that Tudno lived in the fifth or sixth century, when everybody almost appeared to have been either a saint or a king. The distinction was a very sharp one, for the saints were very rarely saintly, and the Kings were very wicked, but the Kings did not seem to have dabbled in the practice of writing. That was left to the Saints, one of whom was Gildas, than whom no Saint had a more tiresome command of the language of abuse, which he bestowed freely on the Princes of his time. Modern commentators were inclined to think that one of the Princes whom Gildas thought fit to scold, lived near Llandudno. Gildas, writing in Latin, spoke of this Prince as "Ursus" (a bear), and some thought they detected in that bear an allusion to Arthur, as the first part of his name coincided with the Welsh Arth (a bear). However that might be, the place mentioned was designated "receptaculum ursi" (the stronghold or refuge of the bear), which he would put back into Archaic Welsh, as Di'n Arth, and possibly that was the farm house in the district called Dinerth. Among other ancient names, here might be mentioned Bod Ysgallen and Gloddaeth, borne by two of the charming residences of the Mostyns. He had no idea what Gloddaeth meant, but possibly it refers to "cloddio" or digging for copper, which Lord Mostyn had mentioned to him as probably dating from Roman times. Bod Ysgallen looked more transparent. Bod usually meant home or residence, and he was inclined to think that Ysgallen had no reference to Ysgall (thistles), but was a modified form of the Goidelic personal name Scantan, of which they had another variant in Ysgolau, a Goidel. As to Deganwy, it was mentioned in the 9th Century as Decantorum, which he would like to emendate into Decantorium, which would exactly correspond to the present name. Later, it was burnt by lightning and afterwards destroyed by the Saxons, in a record of which it was called Arx Decantorum, the Acropolis or stronghold of the Decanti, who bore practically the same name as the Decantæ of Scotland mentioned by Ptolemy in the second century. Proceeding, the speaker stated that the Roman form of Conway was Canovium or Canovio as spelt on an old Roman mile-stone found about eight miles from Caerhun, which was supposed to be the station called Canovium, the real name of Conway being Aber Conway.

Letter of William Morgan, Bishop of St. Asaph, to Sir John Wynn, of Gwydir :—

15 Ffebr., 1603.

Youre moty wes that I shold confyrme youre Lease upon the Rectorye of Llanrwst are dyverse which are enumerated, and when he comes to No. 9 the Bp. says : "My sundrie promysses that youre Lease shold be the fyrst. And one thynge moveth me agaynst all these, viz., my conscience, which assureth me that that youre request ys such that in grauntyng yt I shold prove myselfe an unhonest, unconscionable and irreligouse man : ye a sacrilegiouse robber of my church —a perfydiouse Spoyler of my Diocese and an unnaturall hyndrer of preachers and good scholers : -the consyderatione whereof wold be a contynual terror and torment to my conscience.

And then he goes on to say, "And to com to youre motyve reasons," which he gives in detail, 9 in number, finishing thus, "Amongest other youre kyndnesses, youe gave good testymonie of me. I pray you lette me continewe worthie of yt. So manie chypps have bene all readye taken from the Church, that yt ys readye to fall. God hath blessed youe so well that youe are bownde rather to helpe hys poore Church then to hynder yt. This wth my hartiest commendations to youre selfe and good Mystres Wyn. I reast,

We are youre owne in ye Lord,

WILLM. ASAPHEN.

[To the Right Wor. his Veary loving Friend,
John Wyn of Gwedur, Esquier.]

Wm. Morgan, was Vicar of Welshpool, and afterwards had Llanrhaiadr Mochnant. He was made Bishop of Llandaff in 1595, and translated in 1601 to St. Asaph, where he died in 1604. Bp. Morgan, encouraged by Archbishop Whitgift, published the Welsh Version of the Old and New Testament.

Answer to the answer :—

Hominibus ingratis loquimini, lapides. (To ungrateful men, speak ye, O stones. The sower went out to sowe ; and some of his seede fell in stonie ground, where hitt wythered, because hitt could take noe roote. The seede was good, but the land nought). I may justly say soe to you. I have in all shewed my selfe your ffreinde, in soe much as yf I had not pointed you the waye with my finger (whereof I have yett good testimonye) you had been still Vycar of Llanrhayder. You pleade conscience when you should geve, and make no bones to receave curtesie of your freinds. But I appeale to him that searcheth the conscience of all men, whether your have used me well, and whether hitt be conscience (wch you have ever in your mouth) be the sole hinderance of my request. I will avowe and justifiie hitt before the greatest Dyvyns in England, that it hath been, nowe ys and ever wylbe, that a man may wth a saefe conscience be far mour of a lyvinge, prayeing in effect for the same as much as hitt ys woorth; and soe ys this, surmyse you the value to be as you loyst. Nether was the losse of the thynge that I regard a bodkyn, but your unkinde dealinge. Hitt shall leson me to expect noe sweete fruite of a sower stocke. Your Verball love I esteeme as nothinge: and I make no doubt (wth God's good favour) to lyve to be able to pleasure you as much as you shall me, et E' contra'. You byd me thanke God for his meny benefytts towards me. God graunt me the grace ever soe to doe. In truth, I did much thanke Him in mynde to see you preferred to the place you are in, as yf you had beene my owne brother; but that I recall, for I never expect good wyll of you, nor good torne by you.

JOHN WYN OF GWYDER.

Gwyder, the house that did you
and your's good. 24th February, 1603.
To the Reverend Father the
Lord Busshop of St. Asaphe.

William Morgan, Bishop of St. Asaph to Sir John Wynn of Gwydir :—

Salutem in C.H.R.O.

Seeinge you can better agree with my tithe in Llangustenyn then with me, and have as I heare taken order for the gatheringe of it ; I am loath to contrarie you therein, soe that you send me the money by this bearer for the same, although I know my tithe to be worthe twise as much as you pay for it. But I pray you to cause the tithe of Bodescallan to be gathered in kind : for yor cosen Hugh Gwynne Gru : hath written to me that he would tithe it in specie this yeare.

Thus wishinge you in all thinges the direction of the Holy Ghost, I rest,

Yor sickly neighbour,

WILLM. ASAPHEN.

At St. Asaph the 24th July, 1604.
To his wors. neighbour
John Wynne, of Gwydir, Esquire.

Bp. Wm. Morgan was succeeded by Richard Parry in the see of St. Asaph, who wrote to Sir John Wynn of Gwydir :—

Good Mr. Gwyn,

.   .   .   .

Your hard censure of mye predecessor I am verye sorye to heare : I willinglye embrace nothinge :—De Mortuis nisi sanctum (concerning the dead nothing but what is holy), Domino suo stetit aut cecidit (To His Lord he hath stood or fallen), so doe we. God graunt we may stand unto the Lord unto whose defence I commend us : and with my verye hartye commendations to yrselfe, I rest,

Your lovinge frend,

RIC. ASAPHEN.

Gresford, 24th Febr., 1604.
To the R. Woor. Mye Lovinge
frend John Gwyn of Gwyder,
Esquier, these at Gwyder.

Extracts from the "History and Antiquities of the Town of Aberconwy and its neighbourhood," by the Rev. Robert Williams, B.A., Christ Church, Oxford, Curate of Llangernyw, 1835:

"Its name Conwy, or more properly Cynwy, is derived from *Cyn* chief, and *wy* water and it is allowed to be one of the finest of its length in Europe. The earliest author who makes mention of any place in this neighbourhood, is Tacitus, whose *Cangorum* Civitas is fixed by the learned antiquary Humfrey Llwyd at Deganwy.

When the Romans had subdued this country, they also built a town on the Conwy, but its site was at the distance of five miles higher up the river at Caer-Rhûn (so called from Rhûn,—the son of Maelgwyn Gwynedd,—who subsequently resided there). Its name of Conovium was, according to their general practice, the Latinised form of the Welsh term Cynwy. Conovium was twenty-four miles from Segontium or Caernarvon, and nineteen from Varæ, in the neighbourhood of the present Bodfari.

Early in the 6th Century, Maelgwyn Gwynedd, who had his *Llys* (Court) at Bryn Euryn, fortified Dyganwy, and built there a strong castle. After the death of his father Caswallon, he held his Court here, and in some records he is called King of Dyganwy. Maelgwyn, who succeeded his father Caswallon A.D. 517 in the sovereignty of Gwynedd, was elected King of the Britons, in A.D. 546, on the death of King Arthur. He died of the *Vad Velen* or yellow plague, in the Church of Llanrhos, whither he had taken himself for shelter. The British poets personified disease, and this, in the form of a woman, was to slay Maelgwyn, if he looked upon it, which he incautiously did through the window. Taliesin's prophetic words are these :—

"A strange creature will come from the Marsh of Rhianedd to punish the crimes of Maelgwyn Gwynedd: its hair, its teeth, and its eyes are yellow, and this will destroy Maelgwyn Gwynedd.

The pestilence which raged in the district between the Conway and Dyffryn Clwyd is recorded in the following triad :—

"The three dreadful pestilences of the Isle of Britain. First, the pestilence from the carcases of the Gwyddelians (Irishmen) who were slain in Manuba after they had opposed the county of Gwynedd for twenty-nine years. Second, the pestilence of the yellow plague of Rhos, and which was caused by the carcasses of the slain, and whoever went within reach of the effluvia fell dead immediately. And the third was the pestilence of the fetid sweat, in consequence of the corn having been injured by wet in the time of the oppression of the Normans by William the Bastard."

Dyganwy continued to be the residence of the Kings of North

*The "Cangi" were herdsmen.

Wales till A.D. 810, in the reign of Cynan Tindaethwy, when it was destroyed by lightning, and the town of Aberconwy (Conway) was built out of its ruins. The ruins now remaining are probably those of a castle originally built by Hugh Lupus. Robert of Rhuddlan, who had obtained a grant of several places in the neighbourhood of Rhuddlan from the earl, was probably the constable of this castle for his patron, at the time of his death, which happened on the third of July, 1088. The castle was demolished about a century afterwards by Llewelyn the Great.

In 1210 Randle Blondevil, Earl of Chester, rebuilt the castle of Dyganwy, upon which Llewelyn entered the territories of the Earl, and, having laid them waste, returned home with great booty.

The continued successes of Llewelyn against his enemies and the grievous complaints made by the Marchers, at last excited the King (John) to endeavour to redress his subjects, and, with a large army, he came to Chester, fully determined to execute his vengeance on the inhabitants of this country, and not to leave one alive. In the meantime, Llewelyn, aware of his inability to meet the enemy in the field, had commanded his subjects on the east side of the Conway, in the present counties of Flint and Denbigh, to remove their cattle and other effects to the fastnesses of the Snowdon Mountains ; and King John, meeting with no opposition, advanced along the coast to Rhuddlan, and thence to the Castle of Dyganwy, where he encamped for some time to refresh his wearied army. This event took place in 1211. As he could only depend on having supplies from England, his forces were soon reduced to the greatest straits and misery by the policy of Llewelyn, who had taken possession of the intervening country, and thereby cut off all his resources. All the defiles in the neighbourhood were also in the possession of the Welsh, who slew all that straggled beyond the precincts of the camp. The English, having subsisted for some time upon the flesh of their horses, and having no alternative, made a disgraceful retreat to England, leaving to Llewelyn the task of burying the great number of their dead, who had been starved in the expedition. We find that in the following August, King John, eager to wipe off the stain of his ignominious retreat, entered Wales a second time, and in this expedition, he crossed the Conway and encamped in Arvon; he sent part of his forces to Bangor, which they burnt to the ground, and took the Bishop prisoner. A reconciliation, however, took place through the instrumentality of the Princess Ioan, who was King John's daughter, and was married to Llewelyn ; the English King then retired to England with honour, and greater success than he had gained before.

In 1213, Owen, the son of David ab Owen Gwynedd, had a grant from King John of the three Cantrevs (Hundreds) of Rhos, Rheveiniog, and Dyffryn Clwyd, excepting the castle of Gannock or Dyganwy, and the territory of Creiddyn, where the castle stood. But Owen, together with his father David, soon after met with the reward of his ingratitude and treason, being killed by Prince Llewelyn at Conway.

In the following year, King John having inhumanly murdered the Welsh hostages in his power, who were the sons of our nobility, twenty-eight in number, Llewelyn laid siege to the King's castles between the Dee and Conwy, all of which he took, and among the number was the castle of Dyganwy, thereby freeing North Wales from the insupportable tyranny and oppression of the English garrisons. In 1245, when John de Grey of Wilton was constable, Dyganwy was again visited by a Royal army. Henry III. having summoned Prince David, and all the Barons of Wales, to do homage at Westminster, and to answer for the depredations laid to their charge, determined, on their refusal to appear, to carry into effect his intentions of the entire subjugation of Wales; the English Parliament accordingly granted him the necessary supplies, and on this occasion there was an extraordinary assessment of forty shillings for every knight's fee, called the Scutage of Gannock (Dyganwy). All his Barons, and others who held of the King by knights service, and serjeantry, were summoned to attend him to Wales. Having completed all his formidable preparations, the King advanced as far as Dyganwy with a great army of English and Gascons (inhabitants of an old French province), fully purposing to slay all the inhabitants and to destroy the country. Although he reached this place unmolested, he dared not venture to cross the Conway and follow the Welsh into the mountains of Snowdon. He accordingly halted, and during the ten weeks that he remained here, his army, by reason of their great numbers, was encamped without the walls, and was exposed to many inconveniences; the soldiers suffered greatly from being thinly clad and having no other coverings than tents made of linen. They were also greatly harassed, and their numbers reduced, by the incessant attacks of the Welsh, who cut off all stragglers and endeavoured to storm their camp. The intervening country being again in possession of the Welsh, and all intercourse with England prevented, the King and his army were reduced to a most deplorable state of famine. Some of the events which occurred here at this period and the miseries they suffered are told in the following letter, written by a courtier in the camp to a friend in England:—

The king, with the army is encamped at Gannock (Dyganwy), and is busy in fortifying that place (sufficiently strong already) about which we lay in our tents, in watching, fasting, praying, and freezing. We watch for fear of the Welsh, who were used to come suddenly upon us in the night time : we fast for want of provision—the halfpenny loaf being now risen and advanced to five pence : we pray that we may speedily return safe and scot-free home : and we freeze for want of winter garments, having but a thin linen shirt to keep us from the wind. There is a small arm of the sea under the castle where we lay, which the tide reached, by the conveniency of which, many ships bring us provisions and victuals from Ireland and Chester : this arm lies betwixt us and Snowden, where the Welsh are encamped, and is in breadth, when the tide is in, about a bow-shot. Now it happened, that upon the Monday before Michaelmas-day, an Irish vessel came up to the mouth of the haven, with provision to be sold to our camp, which being negligently looked to by the mariners, was upon the low ebb stranded on the other side of the castle, near the Welsh. The enemy, perceiving this, descended from the mountains, and laid siege to the ship, which was fast upon the dry sands ; whereupon we detached in boats three hundred Welsh of the borders of Cheshire and Shropshire, with some archers and armed men, to rescue the ship : but the Welsh, upon the approach of our men, withdrew themselves to their usual retirements in the rocks and the woods, and were pursued for about two miles by our men on foot, who slew a great number of them. But in their return back, our soldiers, being too covetous and greedy of plunder, among other sacrilegious and profane actions, spoiled the Abbey of Aberconwy, and burnt all the books and other choice utensils belonging to it. The Welsh being distracted at these irreligious practices, got together in great number, and in a desperate manner setting upon the English, killed a great number of them, and following the rest to the water-side, forced as many as could not make their escape into the boats, to commit themselves to the mercy of the waves. Those they took prisoners they thought to reserve for exchange, but hearing how we put some of their captive nobility to death, they altered their minds, and in a revengeful manner scattered their dilacerated carcases along the surface of the water. In this conflict, we lost a considerable number of our men, and chiefly those under the command of Richard, Earl of Cornwall ; as Sir Alan Buscell, Sir Adam de Maio, Sir Geoffry Estuemy, and one Raimond a Gascoign, with about an hundred common soldiers. In the meantime, Sir Walter Bisset stoutly defended the ship till midnight, when the tide returned:

whereupon the Welsh, who assailed us on all sides, were forced to withdraw, being much concerned that we had so happily escaped their hands. The cargo of this ship was three hundred hogsheads of wine, with plenty of other provision for the army, which at that time it stood in very great need of. But the next morning when the sea was returned, the Welsh came merrily down again to the ship, thinking to surprise our men, but as luck would have it, they had at full sea the night before relinquished the ship, and returned safe to the camp. The enemy missing our men, set upon the cargo of the ship, carried away all the wine and other provisions, and then, when the sea began to flow, they set fire to the vessel and returned to the rest of the army. And thus we lay encamped in great misery and distress for want of necessaries, exposed to great and frequent dangers, and in great fear of the private assaults and sudden incursions of our enemies. Oftentimes we set upon and assailed the Welsh, and in one conflict we carried away a hundred head of cattle, which very triumphantly we conveyed to our camp. For the scarcity of provisions was then so great, that there remained but one hogshead of wine in the whole army, a bushel of corn being sold for twenty shillings, a fed ox for three or four marks, and a hen for eight pence : so that there happened a very lamentable mortality, both of man and horse, for want of necessary sustenance of life."

Having undergone such miseries, as are here described, King Henry found his position no longer tenable and he accordingly retreated with his army, without having performed any of his intentions, or having gained the least advantage.

The succeeding Prince of Wales, Llewelyn ab Grufudd, in 1258 having successfully carried his arms into Cheshire, caused King Henry a second time to invade Wales with an immense army ; for he had brought together the whole strength of England : he advanced, without opposition, to Dyganwy, but his further progress, and stay for any length of time, was prevented by the skill of Llewelyn, who had conveyed to the other side of the river all manner of provision and forage, and had secured all the narrow passages, where the English might have crossed the river. Henry was again compelled to make an inglorious retreat, not without suffering a considerable loss.

In 1262 the Castle of Dyganwy, which was of so much importance to the English, and so dangerous to the safety of Wales, was taken and totally demolished by Llewelyn.

The English monarch, irritated by the loss of Dyganwy, determined now to send his son Edward with an army against Llewelyn;

for Dyganwy, being situated on the coast, was open to receive a continual supply of soldiers and provision ; and commanding one of the principal passes of Wales, its garrison was frequently enabled to cut off the excursionary parties of the Welsh ; being likewise a place of great strength in point of structure and situation, it afforded the English a secure retreat upon any disaster. Llywelyn having retired to the west side of the Conwy, Edward, who found it too difficult an attempt to follow him into Snowdon, withdrew his forces ; and the pretext of his retreat was a recall by his father on an affair of importance. In 1277, the King of England, having subdued the intervening country, advanced at the head of a large army into Conwy, where he remained quiet, fully determined to starve Llewelyn into submission. The latter having no resources, for Anglesey, the granary of Wales, was in the hands of the English, was at length compelled, for the sake of his suffering people, to propose an accommodation with Edward ; a peace was accordingly concluded on the most mortifying terms, and afterwards ratified in the King's absence, by the Commissioners of the two Princes at Aberconwy. For some years Llewelyn submitted to the ungenerous and atrocious insults offered him by the English King ; but in 1282, the patience of the Welsh being totally exhausted, they rose in arms, and endeavoured to obtain some alleviation of their miseries. Edward eagerly seized the opportunity of destroying Llewelyn, and joining Wales to England ; about the 1st of Nov. he left Rhuddlan, and advanced with his army to Aberconwy, where he stationed it in advantageous positions in the neighbourhood ; and Edward was here when he had the satisfaction of receiving the head of his brave but unfortunate antagonist, who had been slain at Buallt. Having at length obtained the object of his ambition by the entire conquest of Wales, he annexed this country to the Crown of England. He completed the building of the Castle in 1284, and surrounded the town with walls ; and fearing to trust within them, the members of the Abbey which had been founded here by Llewelyn ab Iorwerth, he removed them to his new foundation at Maenan, near Llanrwst. Although the present town of Aberconwy was enlarged and fortified by Edward the First, we know it was a place of some importance previously ; we have no record relating to the town which arose after the destruction of Dyganwy, except that there was a fortress here called Caer Gyffin, from the rivulet adjoining, built by Maelgwyn Gwynedd in the sixth century, and that the town was also called Aberconwy, for we have the Charter granted by Llewelyn to the Abbey here, which is witnessed and dated from Aberconwy in 1198.

Edward left a strong garrison in the Castle, and made the town a free borough, ordering that the Constable for the time being should be Mayor, and assigning it considerable privileges. William Sikun was first appointed to that office.

There are some very curious conditions mentioned in the Charter, amongst others " that Jews dwell not in the same borough at any time."

The Charter was "given under our hand at Flynt 8th day of September in the twelfth year of our reign."

In the 18th year of his reign, he granted that the burgesses of Aberconwy should be quit of toll, throughout the Kingdom.

In 1290, the Welsh again rose up in arms against the authority of Edward, under Madog, a son of Prince Llewelyn. Alarmed at a revolt which was now rising into importance, and which menaced the safety of his new dominions, Edward came to North Wales to conduct the war in person. Having proceeded in his march to Conwy, he crossed that arm of the sea with a part of his forces ; and returning into the Castle waited for the remainder of his army to follow. But a sudden rise in the Conwy preventing his troops from passing the river, rendered Edward's situation exceedingly alarming ; he was obliged to eat salted meat, in common with the soldiers, and to use water likewise for his drink mixed with honey. The Conway however suddenly subsiding, his forces were enabled to cross the water and come to his relief. The Welsh then abandoned the siege and retired to the mountains of Snowdon. The English King, on the enemy's retreat, passed the Christmas holidays without molestation in the Castle of Conwy.

In 1301 the English Prince of Wales, afterwards Edward II., came down to Aberconwy.

Edward II. granted to the burgesses their town and hamlets.

Edward III. received 20 shillings fine for the confirmation of their Charter.

Richard II. A fine was again paid by the burgesses for the confirmation of the Charter of their Liberties.

In 1399, the unfortunate King Richard retired to Aberconwy, and shut himself up in the Castle, but, finding himself almost alone, he sent word by one of his attendants that he was ready to submit to reasonable terms, and the Archbishop of Canterbury, and Percy, Earl of Northumberland, were immediately despatched by the Duke of Lancaster to know his intentions. The King was however caught in a wily and iniquitous snare, and accompanied Northumberland out of the gate, and when he had reached Penmaen Rhos, he saw a band of soldiers bearing the banners of Percy.

The King found himself betrayed, and was taken prisoner to Flint Castle, where he was delivered into the cruel hands of the Duke of Lancaster.

At the time of Owain Glyndwr's insurrection, in the beginning of the 15th century, John de Masey was Constable of Conway Castle; he had fifteen men at arms and sixty archers with him; 39s. 2d. were allowed to maintain this fortress per day, amounting in the year to £714 15s. 10d.

In 1404, Henry de Scharisbree, Lieutenant of Conway Castle, wrote three letters to William Venables, of Kinderton, Constable of Chester, and Roger Brescy, giving some historical accounts of a period, of which our records are extremely scanty.

The above letters were written about the year 1404. Richard III., in the first or second year of his reign, granted to "Thomas Tunstall, Esqr., the office of Constable of the Castel of Conway, and to have under him the number of twenty-four soldiers for the time of his life, and to have for every of the said soldiers 4d. by the day."

Henry VII., a fine of twenty shillings was paid into the Hanaper Office, for the confirmation of divers liberties and franchises granted by the King and his predecessors. The Charter was again confirmed by Henry VIII., 1 Edward VI., and 3 Elizabeth.

The town of Aberconwy had obtained the great privileges mentioned above from Edward I., in order that he might have a body of Englishmen to maintain his power in Wales; all that held office in his towns of Aberconwy, Beaumaris, and Caernarvon were exclusively English; in course of time, however, some Welshmen crept into office, which the English Burgesses looked upon as an infringement of their rights, considering Wales as a foreign country subjected to the English, but the inhabitants by no means entitled to have any share of the advantages of their own land. They accordingly presented a memorial to the King and his Parliament, which shows the jealous feelings entertained by the two nations towards each other. The memorial refers to the Englishe Waled Towne of Conwey in Northwalles, and prays the King in his present Parliamente to order and redresse that the Burgesses may have theire liberties whole and firme without interrupcion as they and there ancestors have had heretofore : that the said English townes Conwey, Carnarvon, and Bewmares, upon the comone weele of Northwales, shall also be in decaye yf the rule and governance of the same shall goe out of the Englishe men's hands : also that the Captaines of the said Castells be meere Englishmen, and kepe Englishe shouldiours, and not borne in the

Cuntery; also that, according to the Statute of Rutland, and Ordinance of Northwales, Welshmen shall purchase no land within the Englishe towne or ffrancheze of the same, so that the tenants inhitants of the Comotes of Crythyn, &c., shall come everye fridaie with their victailes and Corne to the markett of Conwey as was of old tyme ordeined for the sustentacion of the said Castell and Town: also that noe ale or wyne sould by retaile within viii. leuges of the said towne: that the porter of Conwey, which is nowe a Welshman, may be put out, and the office given to an Englishe Burgesse inhiting in the said Towne for by the Welshe officers the towne hath ofte been Destroied, for it is no more meete for a Welshman to beare any office in Wales, or especiallie in any of the Three englishe Townes then it is for a frinchman to be Officer in Calis or a skotte in Barwicke. . . . Also that noe Capitall officer to the King's grace or to any other lord or Lordes in Northweles shall brue alle to sell or retaile anie wynes in any place of Northweles.*

In 1607, the town was almost depopulated by the plague, and numbers of people were buried in the streets, their bones are frequently found there, when making sewers, and also without the Town Walls. The pestilence was observed to break out here within three weeks of the time it appeared in London; and it must have reached this place so soon owing to the connection of the inhabitants with England. During the civil wars in the reign of Charles I., the importance of Conwy was duly esteemed, and it again became the scene of contention. The most conspicuous character in the history of the town at this period, was a native of the place, namely, the Archbishop of York. He was born in Aberconwy on the 25th day of March, 1582. In the difficulties which arose in consequence of Parliament taking up arms against the King, the Archbishop was compelled to leave his diocese, and he came to his native town of Conwy in 1642. A few months after this, Colonel Mitton with a Parliamentary army came from Chester to Conwy: terms were arranged, and Mitton's army, assisted by the Archbishop in person, who was wounded in the neck, forced open the gates and took the town by storm on the 15th of August, 1646. All the Irish found here were seized by Mitton's command, and being tied back to back, were thrown into the river. The Archbishop expired at Gloddaeth on the anniversary of his birthday, the 25th of March, 1650, in the sixty-eighth year of his age. His body was conveyed to Penrhyn and buried in the Church of Llan-

---

* The Englishmen did not brew good ale: " Cwrw Aberconwy goreu pei pellaf:" " Aberconwy ale, the further off the better," says the old proverb.

degai. There is little to be recorded in the history of Conwy after that time, besides the dismantling of the Castle by the Earl of Conwy. In 1665, the Earl of Conwy stript the Castle of all the timber, iron, and lead, and shipped it off to Ireland; his orders were so rigorously carried into effect, that the smallest particle of iron cannot be found remaining in any part of the Castle.

The Abbey of Aberconwy was honoured by being the burial place of several illustrious persons : of its founder, Llewelyn the Great, whose coffin was removed after the dissolution, and is preserved in the Church of Llanrwst ; it is made of stone, and the sides are curiously carved into quatrefoils. This Prince died in 1240. Previously to him, in 1200, Gruffydd ab Cynan ab Owen Gwynedd was buried here in a monk's cowl, a mode of burying lately introduced from England, and very much practised by the higher ranks, as highly conducive to future bliss ; it may be observed, that about this period, several superstitious practices of the Church of Rome gained ground in Wales, and soon began to corrupt the purity of the ancient British Church.

In 1243, the Abbots of Aberconwy and Cymer, in a dispute between Prince Dafydd (son of Llewelyn the Great) and King Henry III., had commission from the Pope to absolve their Prince from his allegiance to the King of England.

Edward I., after the conquest of Wales, not wishing to have the Abbey in his new English town of Aberconwy, removed it in 1289 to Maenan, about 10 miles higher up the river. Of the original Abbey in Aberconwy there are now no remains.

The walls which surround the town were built the same time as the Castle, and are nearly triangular, almost in the shape of a harp ; in a circuit of about a mile and a quarter there are 21 strong towers. The oldest stone house is that known by the name of the College, which has a singular window fronting the Castle Street, and the sculptured ornaments beneath are unusual ; among them an eagle pouncing upon a child, and coats of arms, relating to the great family of Stanley and others. This was built in the reign of Elizabeth. In the High Street is a large pile of building called Plas Mawr, or the great mansion ; above the entrance the arms of England are carved. The towns of Carnarvon, Beaumaris, and Conwy, enjoyed in consequence of their many privileges, great prosperity and opulence, and even within the last two centuries Sir John Wynne of Gwydir mentions, that they were called the lawyers of Carnarvon, the merchands of Beaumaris, and the gentlemen of Conwy. The weekly market is held on Friday, when no one ought to sell before the bell is rung by one of the sergeants at mace. The

Fairs are held seven times in the year, and are or ought to be opened by the members of the Corporation, who proceed with their wands to the top of the street and read the proclamation, written in 1590. The Fair in September is called the Honey Fair.

Before the passing of the Reform Bill (1832), Conway was a contributory borough in returning a Member to Parliament; this privilege it still retains.

The seal of the Corporation bears the inscription :—

E : D E : Conewey + Sy: Provestri.

Which means :

Edwardus : dedit : Conewey + Sigillam : Provestri.
" Edward gave Conwy the seal for the Provost."

THE CHURCH

was once conventual, and contains a very fine old screen of ornamented wood, above which was the organ loft, now removed. There is a very curious monument of Nicholas Hookes, who lies buried in the Chancel, with the inscription :—

" Here lyeth ye body of Nichs. Hookes of Conway Gen. who was ye 41st child of his Father Wm. Hookes Esqr. by Alice his wife, and ye Father of 27 children, who dyed ye 20th Day of March, 1637."

Amongst the customs of the town which used to be observed from time immemorial was one that went by the name of *stocsio*,— putting in the stocks. On Easter Sunday, crowds of boys and men proceeded with wands of gorse to proclaim on Pentwthil (the town mountain) the laws and regulations, which were to be observed on the following morning. The bridegroom who was last married, was always sought for to perform the office of Crier ; mounted on a heap of stones, he proclaimed the notices to the effect that all men under 60 years of age were to appear in the street before 6 o'clock on the following morning, and all under 40 before 4, and all under 20 not to go to bed at all under penalty of being put in the *stocks*. At an early hour in the morning, the stocks were placed at the bottom of the street, and a party headed by a fife and drum band proceeded with a cart to convey dilinquents to the place of punishment. The culprit being arrested and having time allowed him to dress, if caught in bed, was placed in the cart and triumphantly hurried to the stocks, where one of the party, having secured his feet, gave him a lecture upon the heinousness of idleness and breaking an old-established custom; then, taking hold of his right hand, he asked him a few questions such as these:— Whether he likes better the mistress or the maid,—ale or buttermilk,—whether he would go through the gate of a field if open, or over the stile, &c. If in his answers he fixed upon what was obviously preferable, his hand was the more thickly covered with some dirty mud, and he was then released with cheers. This sport was continued with the greatest good humour until 8, when the rest of the day was spent at playing at ball in the Castle.

CREIDDYN.

The land to the east of Aberconwy, between the river and the sea is called Creiddyn, a name derived from its form (what juts into), It is a Cwmwd or Commol in the Cantref (Hundred) of Rhos, but in the County of Caernarvon, it contains the three parishes of Llangystenin, Eglwys Rhos, and Llandudno, and it is bounded on every side by water, except the south, where the parishes of Llansantffraid glan Conwy and Llandrillo-yn-Rhos adjoin.

PRE-ROMAN RELICS IN CREIDDYN.

A very interesting discovery of pre-Roman ornaments and bronze weapons, according to the *Weekly News* of May 20th, 1898, was recently made at Llandudno. Two youths resident at Brankleigh, Craigydon, named Lewis and Arthur Riddell, were out for a ramble on the Great Orme's Head, when they discovered, amongst the *debris* at the back of a large loose rock near the Pigeons' Cave, two Decantean shoulder brooches, together with a bronze "celt" (or head of a battle-axe), and a socketted dart-point (probably unique), also of bronze. One of the brooches (both of which are hollow, of fine gold, and in breadth about the diameter of a penny), weighs nearly three-quarters of an ounce, and is beautifully engraved with twenty-one concentric lines, whilst the other bears traces of having been enamelled. An antiquarian conjecture is that their original owner, a Pictish chieftain, lost his life and sword in battle, whereupon a fellow-Decantean tribesman hid his remaining weapons and ornaments, and, for some reason, never returned for them. The value of the gold brooches (which are of the pinless shape used amongst the early Celtic peoples to gather the corners of the robes together, the under robe being thus secured on the right shoulder, and the outer robe on the left shoulder) proves that the owner was a man of considerable position and wealth. The celt, it may be interesting to add, weighs thirteen ounces; and the dart-point, one ounce. Prior to the Roman conquest, the territory of the Decantæ included the entire Creiddyn peninsula and environs, their boundary on the Conway River being situate near Hendre-waelod, Glanconway. Several somewhat similar "celts" were found at Deganwy some years back. The value of the present find consists in the bronze-age shoulder-brooches, extremely few of which are known as being still in existence. It has been suggested that the relics should be bought for the new local museum which is ere long to be constituted in Conway Castle.

THE RIVER CONWAY.

The River Conway was at one time noted for its Pearl Fishery, which it is said attracted the notice of the Romans. Pliny says that Julius Cæsar dedicated to one of the Temples in Rome (Venus Genetrix) a breastplate set with British pearls, probably from Conway. Mr. Bridge of Conway (he died in 1886), asserted that in the year 1851 he paid nearly £200 to the poor people of the neighbourhood for collecting them. One of the finer kind of Conway pearls was presented to Catherine, Queen of Charles II., by Her Majesty's Chamberlain, Sir Robert Wynne, of Gwydir, and honoured with a place in the Royal Crown, which it probably yet adorns, in testimony of the gallant Welshman's loyalty. During the reign of George III., Sir Richard Vaughan appeared at Court with a button and loop in his hat set with Conway pearls. Miss Catherine Sinclair, in her own pleasant fashion, says, when she was at Conway (in 1833) "unluckily we had not time to wait until a necklace could be collected. The imitation ones are so excellent, however, that it was less to be regretted. Even Oriental pearls are scarcely to be distinguished from those which originate in Bond Street, and the celebrated fringe worn by Mrs. Warren Hastings, which used to occasion so much discussion, would hardly be more noticed now than if they were peas. The Duchess of Ormond formerly offered £80 to purchase a peculiarly fine Conway pearl; and they were often sold for four guineas each, when the colour was good. It is said that nothing preserves pearls so perfectly white as being constantly worn, and that the Roman ladies, conscious of this, always slept in theirs. Conway pearls are mentioned by Spencer in the "Fairy Queen":—

"Conway which out of his streame doth send
Plenty of pearls to deck his dames withal."

THE PEARL FISHERY OF CONWAY.

In our contemporary, *The Queen*, Sir Walter Besant, in his fascinat'ng series of notes entitled "The Voice of the Flying Day," recently referred to this subject as follows:—"The Pearl Fishery of Conway seems to interest many readers, if one may judge from the letters received. The following information, the last I can promise on the subject, will enable everybody to go off fishing for themselves. There are two kinds of mussels found in the Conway river. The first, which is rare, is five and a half inches long by two and a half inches broad. The pearl found in this kind is said to be very fine, and in size and quality not inferior to the Oriental pearl. The other kind is much smaller ; it is found in great quantities on the bar of the river, where it used to be gathered by the sackful at low tide. The sacks were then carried to a place where great iron pots filled with water were hung up over fires. Here the mussels were boiled. The fish were then taken out and put into a tub, where they were stamped with bare feet till they were reduced to pulp; water was then poured in; the animal matter floated, the sand and pearls sank to the bottom; when the pearls had been collected they were sold to the trade at a price varying from eighteenpence to three shillings an ounce. Nobody, it is added, ever knew what became of these pearls. *Weekly News*, March, 1898.

The River Conway is also famous for its *brwyniaid*, or sparlings, which pay their visit in January and February; they spawn in March and April, after which they depart, their stay seldom exceeding four weeks. They vary in size, but rarely do they exceed a foot in length or more than half-a-pound in weight. It is a fish of beautiful form and colour, the head being transparent and the skin so thin, that with a microscope, the blood may be observed to circulate. They have a very peculiar scent, which is compared to cucumber or violet, but more properly to rushes, and their Welsh name *brwyniaid* is derived from *brwyn*, rushes, owing to this circumstance.

LLANSANTFFRAID.*

In this Parish not far from Hendrewaelod, is a very large Cromlech.† This Cromlech is known by the name of Allor Moloch‡ (Moloch's altar); it consists of five upright stones about 3½ feet high, on which rests an immense top-stone,—the greatest length of this is 12ft., breadth 8ft., and the greatest thickness 4ft., its probable weight about 22 tons; behind are two upright stones, each about 9ft. high from the floor of the Cromlech and about 6ft. from each other.

---

* Llansantffraid. A Cromlech, in Archæology, the name given to collections of enormous blocks of rough stone, placed erect upon the ground, and usually arranged in circles. They were, until recently, regarded as places of worship set up by the Celts or Druids; but it appears now to be certain that they are due to the men of the Stone Age, who occupied a great part of Europe at a date far anterior to the Celts, and that they were intended to surround the localities in which that primitive race buried their dead.

† This Church is dedicated to St. Bride or Bridget. On her day, Feb. 1st., the Rector reads prayers; and, out of the offerings of that day, he is paid eighteen-pence,—the Wardens twelve pence, and the clerk six-pence, the rest to the poor. "Attending St. Ffraid's Day" is a frequent entry in the old Parish Books.

‡ I have ascertained from "Benffro," that the remains of the Cromlech "Allor Moloch" still exist, but that the description given by the Rev. Robert Williams in 1835 hardly applies to its present condition (1898). Of the five upright stones mentioned by him, three only now exist—the other two having been cut up by some Vandals, and used as gate posts in an adjoining field. The "Allor" itself has fallen on one side, owing no doubt to the removal of the two stone supports.

In this Parish, Gibson, the eminent sculptor was born; his birthplace is commerated by a stone slab of oblong shape (over the door facing the road) on a house close to the Baptist Chapel, Fforddlas. The house has of course been restored and remodelled. At the time Gibson was born, it was only a thatched cottage, ground floor only. The following is the inscription:—

YN Y TY HWN YN 1789
Y GANWYD JOHN GIBSON R.A.
Y MYNOR–GERFIWR ENWOG
BU FARW YN RHUFAIN
IONR. 27, 1866 YN 77 OED.

There was considerable discussion in the Press some years ago in which " J. D. Ffraid " took a prominent part, as to whether this house *was* the birthplace of John Gibson. There is no doubt as to Gibson's parents having lived there at one time, but the famous sculptor having been baptised in Gyffin Church (near Conway), it has been contended that he was born in the latter parish, subsequent to his father's removal to the post of gardener at Bodlondeb, Conway. I am most credibly informed that the preponderance of the evidence is in favour of the cottage in the parish of St. Ffraid.

LLANDRILLO-YN-RHOS.

On Bryn Euryn (the brow where the sloes grow) was Llys (Court) Maelgwyn Gwynedd, where he resided before he removed to Deganwy. The valley on the South is called NANT SEMPYR, a name supposed to be derived from a Roman General, possibly Sempronius; that the Romans have visited this neighbourhood, is corroborated by a silver coin of Hadrian being dug up in a field here. HADRIANVS AVGVSTVS. Reverse, TRANQVILLITAS AVG COS III. P. P. There are also the remains of an old copper mine, worked by the Romans. Llys Bryn Euryn was the residence of Edneved Vychan, in the beginning of the 13th century, the able minister and general of Llewelyn the Great; having attacked the army of Ranulph, Earl of Chester, and having defeated it with great slaughter, he slew three of the chief commanders, and brought their heads to Prince Llewelyn, who thereupon honoured him with a new achievement, viz., Gules, a chevron ermuie, between three Englishmen's heads, couped proper; which coat his descendants bear ever since. Edneved Vychan " built a chapel and had licence of the Pope for evermore to sing divine service therein for his soul and his ancestors' and progenitors' souls always; and had authority to give his tithes and oblations to his chaplain there serving." The Chapel, built by Edneved, formed

the west half of the north aisle of the present Church, with a small
cupola at the west end ; this side or aisle was afterwards lengthened
by the parishioners when their Church was destroyed by the sea ;
and in the north wall of the old Chapel there are to be seen two
arches, which communicated with Edneved's seat. The south aisle
was built by the ladies Conwy, the descendants of Gruffydd
Goch, lord of Rhos and Rhyfoniog ; and collaterally also of
Edneved ; they were the last occupiers of the Court of Bryn Euryn,
and they left a large sum towards restoring the present handsome
tower. In 1818, when lowering the Churchyard on the south side
of the Church, an immense quantity of bones were discovered
heaped together confusedly : they were most probably conveyed
from the Churchyard of the original Church, which was situated
considerably lower down, at the time it was destroyed by the sea.
At a very low ebb, and when a strong south-west wind prevails,
the waves may be distinctly seen breaking upon a sarn or causeway,
which runs into the sea from Great Orme's Head, about 4 miles
below Llandrillo Church ; and it is still called the " muriau," or the
Walls. Morfa Rhianedd, a great extent of territory, which the sea
has now overwhelmed, reached to an unknown distance below
Abergele and the present shore of the north of Flintshire. Below
the Church, is Rhosfynach, the Marsh or Feu farm of the Monks
(Monachorum) ; there is a very large Weir, which runs from this
point. An exclusive grant of all the fisheries along the coast,
below the Commot of Isdulas, was made to Morgan ab John ab
David, of Maesegwig, an ancestor of the recent proprietor, Thomas
Lewis Parry Evans (deceased), by the great Earl of Leicester, who
had the lordship of Denbigh. This indenture is dated the 30th
June, 17th of Elizabeth.

Near the Weir on the shore is a small structure called Capel
Trillo, or St. Trillo's Chapel, the saint to whom the Church is
dedicated. Its form is oblong, with a small window, or rather
loop-hole, in each side, and at the end a very small doorway and a
stone roof; within is a well of excellent water.* This building is
generally supposed to have been a chapel where prayers were
offered for success in fishing.

---

*Where the pious doubtless assembled in former days to " drink and pray,"
as at the " blessed spring " whence the dying thirst of *Marmion* is slaked :

> " A little fountain-cell,
> Where water, clear as diamond spark,
> In a stone basin fell."

And above which :

> " Some half-worn letters say
> Drink, weary pilgrim, drink and pray

In the Church between the two pointed arches already mentioned, is a tomb stone or lid of a Sarcophagus with the following inscription in Saxon letters, HIC IACET DNS : EDNEVED : DEDYNEYRT : CS AN. PROPIETVR DEVS AMEN.

Dinerth is another name for Llandrillo.

The gwyl mab sant (or Saint's Day) is the 16th of June.

The Rector (Sinecure) and Vicar used to have a share of the tithes of Llanelian, Llysfaen, and Llansantffraid.

LLANGYSTENYN.

This Church is dedicated to Cystennyn, the son of Cynfor ; who was elected to the royal dignity by the Britons about A.D. 390. In Pope Nicholas's taxation in A.D. 1291, it is called a chapel to Abergele.

EGLWYS RHOS.*

On a raised tombstone in the north of the Chancel is the following inscription :—" Here lyeth the Body of Margaret Wynne third daughter of Colonel Hugh Wynne of Bodysgallen (who at his own expense raised a Regiment of Foot for the service of King Charles the First and was a great sufferer for the Royal Cause)."

In this Parish is Penrhyn, which was for several centuries the seat of the family of Pugh, the last of whom married the heiress of Coytmor. Robert Pugh of Penrhyn Creiddyn, was sheriff of Caernarvonshire in 1561. This family was descended from Edneved Vychan, and his arms are carved in stone on the house. The more recent part of the house was built in 1590, according to the date above the fire place. At a short distance from the house, is the family Chapel, now desecrated into a stable ; it is about 25ft. long by 15 wide. The family, for a long period after the Reformation, professed the Roman Catholic religion, and they kept a priest, who officiated in this Chapel for themselves and a few Catholic neighbours ; in connection with this circumstance is the following anecdote, which was current in the neighbourhood : it is said that a plot was formed here to put to death all the Protestants in Creiddyn, and for the accomplishment of this deed a body of men was to arrive at a certain time of the night ; previously to their coming,

---

*Otherwise Llanrhos. The simple name of " Eglwys Rhos " (the Church in the "rhos" or moorland) indicates its early antiquity and its pre-eminence among the Churches of that cantref (hundred) or district when the native Princes of Wales had their residence at Deganwy, within its limits ; just as the other name, " Llanrhos," or, more fully, " Llanfair yn Rhos," i.e., " St. Mary's in Rhos," indicates the influence of the Cistercian monks of Aberconway, who on some occasion of its re-erection dedicated it, as their custom was, in the name of their favorite saint. It was here, at Bodysgallen, that Caswallon-Law-Hir lived, who gave permission to S. Cyndeyrn to settle at Llanelwy ; and in this Church lies buried Maelgwyn Gwynedd, the founder of the see.

great preparations were made in preparing provisions, and a servant of Gloddaith, who paid his addresses to a woman in the service of the family, finding her engaged at an unseasonable hour, obtained by his urgent enquiries a knowledge of the conspiracy ; he immediately hastened home, and disclosed what he had heard to his master, who with the greatest despatch, procured a troop of horse, and invested Penrhyn. This speedy intervention frustrated their designs, and some of the inmates escaped, while others were taken ; but the priest, who was supposed to be the contriver of the plot, for some time eluded the strict search made for him ; it happened however that some persons being in a boat out at sea, observed smoke ascending from Rhiwleden rock, which circumstance exciting their curiosity, they hastened there, and in a small cave called " Ty yn y graig," which is about 90 feet from the summit, and the approach to which is extremely difficult, the priest was dis-covered ; he was drawn and quartered in a field below the house, and his name, Sir William Guy, is even preserved ; there was a hole behind the house called " Twll arfau can' o wyr " (the hole of the arms of a hundred men), where it is supposed that the arms were concealed.

As these traditionary accounts are generally interesting, another still, more curious relating to Penrhyn, the truth of which seems never to have been doubted by the neighbourhood, is here inserted. At the time of the following occurrence, the family at Penrhyn con-sisted of a son and two daughters ; the former, according to the practice of the age, went on his travels abroad ; but before he set out, he took the precaution of putting a needle between one of the joists and the ceiling in the little kitchen, and he also drove the tooth of a harrow into a pear-tree in the orchard. After the lapse of many years, and all hopes of his return being given over, he arrived a beggar, and coming home he found his parents dead, and his sisters in possession of his property. He stated who he was, but the sisters insisted that he was an impostor, asserting that they were certified of their brother's death ; to prove his identity, he said that the needle would be found in a certain place, and as a further proof he named a particular tree into which he had driven the harrow tooth. The needle was found, and when they followed him to the orchard, he removed the bark which had grown over the iron, and showed it to the sisters : notwithstanding he was forcibly ejected from the premises, and it is said he was flogged with a whip, in which large pins were fixed, as an additional punishment of his supposed imposture. He was received into a neighbouring cottage by the inhabitants, who had known him before he went abroad, and were satisfied of his identity ; he remained here for some time ; but having gone out one day, he was missed, and never returned. Although his fate was surmised, no clue could be obtained to what had become of him ; and this mysterious event was constantly talked of by the country, and successively handed down from father to son ; to this cause also, the common people, fond of the marvellous, have assigned the decay of the family, as being under a curse, which had once been of the highest respectability : the estates have long been sold, and the family is now extinct. It is of course always difficult to arrive at the exact date of this sort of traditionary tales ; but probably this occurrence happened about 150 years ago. To make the above account complete, the then tenant of Penrhyn, not many years ago, had occasion to build a lime-kiln, and in a fissure of the rock, filled with soil, he discovered a perfect skeleton, immediately behind the house.

The greater part of the present house of Gloddaith was built by Thomas Mostyn, in the reign of Queen Elizabeth ; but there was a residence here of the ancient family of Gloddaith for several centuries before. In 1448 Gruffydd ab Rhys ab Gruffydd ab Madoc Gloddaith ab Madoc ab Iorwerth Goch of Creiddyn lost seven children in the same week, who died of the plague. By this calamity, Margaret became sole heiress, and her marriage in 1460, with Hywel ab Ievan Vychan of Mostyn, brought the Gloddaith estate to that family, with whom it still continues.

Bodysgallen is a name evidently derived from Bod Caswallon. Near this site was a residence of Caswallon Law Hir (long hand) who succeeded to the sovereignty of North Wales in 443, and died in 517, after enjoying it for the long period of seventy-four years.

The mansion house of Marl was built in 1661 ; the greater portion was destroyed by fire about 155 years ago, which arose from negligence in airing the books.

LLANDUDNO

is the northernmost of the three parishes of Creiddyn, and includes the ruins of Gogarth, a large palace at one time of the Bishops of Bangor.* The Church is dedicated to St. Tudno, who lived in the beginning of the 6th century ; he was one of the sons of Seithenyn, King of the Plain of Gwyddno, whose land was inundated, and he was a Saint of the Bangor Dunod, or the College at Bangor, in Flintshire.

*There is here a relic of Druidical times, the " Maen Sigl," a Logan or rocking stone, called *Cryd Tudno*, St. Tudno's cradle. It is an immense stone, so equally poised that a slight push will put in rocking motion. Puffin Island, Ynys Seiriol, formerly known as Priestholme, is in the County of Flint, to which it is supposed it was once joined by an arm of land running past the Ormsheads from the neighbourhood of Rhyl.

.. Pwllycrochan Hotel, ..

(THE LATE RESIDENCE OF LADY ERSKINE),

⬦ COLWYN BAY.

JOHN PORTER, Proprietor.

THIS First-class Family Hotel is most beautifully situated in its own finely-wooded Park, in the Bay of Colwyn, commanding splendid views; within a short drive of Conway and Llandudno, and a few minutes walk to the Beach and Station. A most desirable winter residence, nicely sheltered, also heated throughout with hot air. To meet the increased demand for accommodation, the Proprietor has added a wing of Sitting and Bedrooms.

SEA BATHING. ∴ LAWN TENNIS.

BILLIARDS, &c.

∴ POST HORSES AND CARRIAGES. ∴

J. W. THOMAS,

Photographer,

KENSINGTON HOUSE, CONWAY ROAD,

COLWYN BAY.

Important to Invalids—Studio on Ground Floor.

VICTOR ALBERT,

Watchmaker, Jeweller and Optician,

CONWAY ROAD, COLWYN BAY.

N.B.—OLD GOLD and SILVER PLATE Bought for Cash.

DICK'S BOOTS

ARE RELIABLE.

The Styles are Perfect. The Prices are Unequalled. Durability and Comfort Combined.

REPAIRS RECEIVE SPECIAL ATTENTION.

DICK'S CASH BOOT STORES,

10, Station Road, COLWYN BAY.

Proprietor: G. F. GUNNER.

LLANDUDNO AND AT COLWYN BAY.

❋ LOCKYER'S ❋

Private Hotels and Boarding Establishments.

NOTED FOR VERY LIBERAL DIET, MODERATE CHARGES, AND ALL HOME COMFORTS.

G. J. LOCKYER, Sole Proprietor.

. . . FOR . . .

STATIONERY .

·.· OF EVERY DESCRIPTION,

R. E. Jones & Bros.,

WEEKLY NEWS OFFICE,

. . . 8, STATION ROAD,

COLWYN BAY.

Printers, Bookbinders,

Booksellers, News Agents.

CIRCULATING LIBRARY.

CASTLE HOTEL,
CONWAY.

FIRST CLASS FOR FAMILIES AND GENTLEMEN.

.. THE AMERICAN HOUSE OF THE ..
DISTRICT.

NEAR THE WORLD-RENOWNED ..

.. OLD CASTLE.

FINE GOLF LINKS.

MISS DUTTON, PROPRIETRESS.

LLANDRILLO-YN-RHOS.

A SOUVENIR.

COMPILED BY

REV. T. E. TIMOTHY

CURATE OF LLANDRILLO-YN-RHOS.

1910.

SHREWSBURY :

L. Wilding, 33 Castle Street.

CONTENTS.

PREFACE.

THIS little 'Souvénir' is an attempt to satisfy a desire for information regarding the Parish of Llandrillo-yn-Rhos, often expressed by residents, and by visitors to this beautiful corner of Wales. I trust that to the parishioners it will be an incentive to take an interest in the historical associations connected with the place they reside in, and that to the visitors it will be a reminder of a pleasant holiday spent at this bracing sea-side resort. The proceeds of the sale of this 'Souvenir' will be given to the Building Fund of a new Church at Rhos; purchasers, who are dissatisfied with the contents, will, therefore, have the satisfaction of knowing that their money has been spent in a good cause.

In the compilation of the historical account of the Parish I have been much assisted by the booklet written by the late Rev. W. Venables Williams, Vicar of this Parish, and the notes by the Rev. Meredith Hughes, Prestatyn, contained therein. Other books that have been consulted are Newell's History of the Welsh Church; Welsh Sketches by E. S. A., published in 1851; Mabinogion, edited by Sidney Lanier: Flamebearers of Welsh History, by Owen Rhoscomyl: and Bingley's 'North Wales.' I have also received information, for which I am grateful, from the Rev. John Fisher, Vicar of Cefn, and Mr. W. Bezant Lowe, Llanfairfechan. The etched illustrations are by Mrs. E. James Evans, Vicarage, Llandrillo-yn-Rhos. The short dramas, 'Ednyfed Fychan,' and 'Olwen of the Monks' Weir' were written for the purpose of providing attractions to Church Bazaars held in the Parish.

Readers desiring information regarding the archæological history of the Churches in Wales, or of the places in the neighbourhood of Aber-Conway are recommended to procure the following books: 'Lives of British Saints,' by Rev. S. Baring-Gould, M.A., and Rev. John Fisher, B.D., and 'The Heart of Northern Wales' (to be published shortly) by W. Bezant Lowe, M.A., F.C.S.

T. E. TIMOTHY,

Llandrillo-yn-Rhos.

May 12, 1910.

BRIEF ARCHÆOLOGICAL HISTORY.

NAME.

The old name by which this parish was known, seems to have been Dinerth or Dynerth or Denyryt. Historical records of the sixth, ninth, and the twelfth centuries refer to this parish as Dinerth Goch Rhufonioc. The derivation of Dinerth is uncertain. It is supposed to be a shortened form of " Din-garth," which means either a mountain-fort, or, a fort with ramparts or earthworks. Professor Rhys of Oxford in an address on place-names suggested that the name is connected with the word ' arth ' the Welsh for bear, and supposed to refer to Arthur, a prince of North Wales, scornfully spoken of by Gildas, the British historian of the sixth century, as ' ursus ' (a bear), the writer, who wrote scathingly concerning the princes of his day, probably playing on this prince's name ' Arth-ur.' Dinerth in this case would mean ' Arthur's fort,' or, ' the fort of the bear.' Whether the word ' arth ' has anything to do with the old name of this parish is problematical, but there is one thing worthy of remark, namely, that from a long distance away, on the Abergele or Conway side of this parish, Bryn Euryn, the hill above the Church, on whose summit are traces of a British fort or encampment, bears a curious resemblance to a crouching animal ; remembering how names are often suggested by the contour of the surrounding country, or by some physical properties of the land, it is not improbable that this prominent hill, whose contour in olden days suggested, perhaps, a crouching bear, may have given rise to the name Dinerth or Dinarth, to signify ' the bear-like fort.' Rhufonioc, now called Rhufoniog, corruptly, for Rhiwoniog, means the hilly country, while 'goch' means red, the colour of the soil ; hence the old name of the parish, which appears in the oldest records, means probably, ' the fort with red earthworks in a hilly country.'

From the year 1291, when the taxation of Pope Nicholas was made, until 1535 there are no historical records of this

parish in existence, and it is supposed that in the interval
between these two dates the name of the parish was changed
into the present one, Llandrillo-yn-Rhos, 'the Church of
Trillo on the plain,'—*llan* signifying an enclosed place, hence a
sacred place, churchyard, or a church; while *rhos* means a
tableland, a plain, or a marsh.

BRYN EURYN.

This prominent hill in the parish from whose summit a
glorious view may be obtained, is supposed to be called after
Euryn, the son of Helig ab Glanawg. Helig lived at one time
at Llys Helig, a palace standing on the land which once
existed between Penmaenmawr and Anglesea, but which was
submerged in the sixth century. Helig became over-lord of
this district about the end of the sixth century. Euryn devoted himself to religion and was known as Euryn y Coed Helig,
Euryn of the willow trees.

The word ' Euryn ' however, may simply be, the word
derived from *aur* (gold), and meaning golden or yellow; hence,
Bryn Euryn would signify the golden or yellow hill, reference
being made to the appearance of the hill when the gorse, which
grows thickly upon it, is in bloom.

MORFA RHIANNEDD.

Included originally in the township of Dinerth was a
portion of a large tract of land, now submerged, but supposed
at one time to have extended from the Great Orme's Head to
the Point of Air in Flintshire. This district was of a low-lying,
marshy nature, and was known as Morfa Rhiannedd or the
marsh of Rhiannedd. It was protected from the sea by dykes.
Traces of these dykes still exist, for, during very low tides,
waves, it is said, can be seen to break in a long line from West
to East about a mile from the shore. The sea has always been
encroaching along this coast, and even now, means have to be
employed to resist its attack, as may be seen from the sea-wall
which borders the road leading to the Little Orme's Head.

It is uncertain as to *when* Morfa Rhiannedd was submerged. In the 6th century it was in existence, because

Taliesin mentions it in his prophecy relating to Maelgwyn Gwynedd, saying :

" Fe ddaw pry rhyfedd, O Forfa Rhiannedd
I ddial anwiredd ar Faelgwyn Gwynedd :
A'i flew, a'i ddannedd, a'i lygaid yn eurydd,
A hyn a wna ddiwedd ar Faelgwyn Gwynedd."

(a strange creature will come from the marsh of Rhiannedd to punish the crimes of Maelgwyn Gwynedd : its hair, its teeth, and its eyes are yellow, and this will destroy Maelgwyn Gwynedd).

Again, if Pennant is right in saying that Richard II. was taken prisoner under the cliff of Penmaenrhos, by the Earl of Northumberland, who then conveyed him to Flint Castle, it is evident that a portion of Morfa Rhiannedd was in existence in the 12th century.

Tradition says that the submergence took place in the 8th or 9th century. The probability is that the submergence was a gradual one, large tracts disappearing, time after time, between the 8th and 13th centuries. It is likely that the old Parish Church, which was situated on this plain, not far from the head of the present Rhos Pier, was destroyed during the later submergences of the 13th century.

That such a district as Morfa Rhiannedd did exist at one time, is proved by the fact that at very low water, trunks of trees have been observed all along this coast : and, that on a tombstone in Abergele Churchyard is an inscription, which (if its statement is to be relied upon) shows that the man whom it commemorates, at one time had his dwelling far out in what is now the Bay of Abergele, which Bay must thus have been formed by a great submergence that had taken place. Unfortunately there is no date on this tombstone, whose inscription runs thus :—

Yma mae'n gorwedd
Yn Mynwent Mihangel,
Gwr oedd ei annedd
Dair milldir ýn y Gogledd.

(Here lies in the Churchyard of St. Michael a man who had his residence three miles to the north).

It may be added too, as a proof that Morfa Rhiannedd did exist, and that its submergence was probably a gradual

one, that when the sewerage pipes in connection with the
Drainage Scheme carried out by the Colwyn Bay Urban
District Council in 1907 were being laid, the Contractor, at a
spot near the lowest water-mark, had to cut through a wall
about six feet in width—evidently an old stone dyke erected
to withstand the sea.

LLYS EURYN.

Almost at the foot of Bryn Euryn stand the ruins of Llys
Euryn (*Euryn's Court or Palace*). The present ruins are those
of the palace built by Ednyfed Fychan in the 13th century.
It was burnt down in 1409 by Owain Glyndwr. The remains
were modernised, and in the 15th century the restored Llys
Euryn was occupied by the Ladies Conwy, the descendants of
Gruffydd Goch, lord of Rhos and Rhufoniog, and from whom
it passed into the Mostyn family. The ruins and the land
adjoining, now belong to Sir Everard Cayley, Bart.

Tradition says that the site of Llys Euryn was also the
site of a palace occupied by Maelgwyn Gwynedd in the 6th
century. Maelgwyn lived in this part before he built the Castle
of Deganwy, where he afterwards resided and held his court.
As Maelgwyn Gwynedd, the most famous of the princes in
Wales in the 6th century, and often spoken of as King Maelgwyn Gwynedd, played an important part in the history of
this neighbourhood, I append a short account of his life.

Maelgwyn Gwynedd lived in the 6th century, the century
known as the " Age of the Saints," and the century which
witnessed the birth of five Bishoprics in Wales, with the found-
ing of two of which Maelgwyn seems to have been closely
connected. It was he who gave St. Kentigern, the founder of
St. Asaph, land whereon to build his Church which occupied
the same site as the present Cathedral, and it was Maelgwyn
who made Bangor, the see of a Bishopric, Deiniol being the
first Bishop. From this, one gathers that Maelgwyn was a
great benefactor of the Church ; and yet, of all the princes
against whose wickedness Gildas, the monk and historian of
the 6th century turns the bitterness of his indignation, Maelgwyn is the subject of the severest invectives and reproaches.
According to Gildas, Maelgwyn, ' the dragon of the island,

who had deprived many princes of their territories and their lives,' was the 'first in evil, greater than many in power and in wickedness, more lavish in giving, more profuse in sins, more powerful in arms and bolder in the destruction of the soul.' From the writings of Gildas we gather that in the 6th century, despite the number of Saints it gave birth to, the princes in Wales almost excelled in wickedness the worst of the kings of Israel and Judah during the periods of the great prophets. Maelgwyn, judging from the account of Gildas and from the writings of the Bards, was evidently a great warrior, a patron of art, and a wicked king who, during fits of repentance sought to buy the favour of heaven, by generous bequests to the Church. He supported over thirty bards at his court in Deganwy. He is supposed to have died in 547 in Llanrhos Church, whither he had retired for shelter and sanctuary, from the Yellow Plague which ravaged Wales during the 6th century, and which is supposed to have originated from the effluvia of the unburied corpses of the slain in a battle fought on Morfa Rhiannedd. This plague is the one referred to by Taliesin in his prophecy in which he personifies the disease by describing it as a creature of yellow eyes, hair and teeth.

Llys Euryn, however, is more famous as the residence of Ednyfed Fychan, who lived there during the latter part of the 13th century. Ednyfed had other residences in Aberffraw in Anglesea, once the seat of the Kings of Wales, and in Bryn Ffanigle in Denbighshire. He is so closely connected with the history of this parish and its Church, that I give a brief account of *his* life too.

Ednyfed Fychan was descended from Marchudd ab Cynan, chief of the tribes of North Wales, who died in 1136, and was buried on the left side of the great Altar at Bangor. Cynan was such a generous benefactor of the Church, that in his day, it is said, North Wales 'glittered with Churches as the firmament with stars.' Ednyfed had many titles and was evidently a man of great ability and prowess. He was Baron of Bryn Ffanigle, Lord of Cricketh, Chief Justice and Prime Minister of Llewellyn ab Iorwerth, or, Llewellyn ein Llyw Olaf (*Llewellyn our last Prince*). On his breast-plate was a Saracen's head, signifying that either he or his ancestors had, at one time, taken part in the Crusades. This device was afterwards changed at the command of his Prince, into that which still distinguishes his descendants, viz., 'Gules between three Englishmen's heads (triphen Sais) couped and Chevron Ermine,' on account of a feat of valour accomplished by Ednyfed, in one of the numerous Welsh wars with the English, when he killed with his own hands three of the chief English nobles under Ranulph of Chester. Ednyfed was the ancestor of Owen Tudor who married Catherine the widow of King Henry V. and whose son Edmund was the father of King Henry VII.

Ednyfed was married twice. His first wife was the daughter of Llyerch ap Bran, by whom he had several children, amongst them being Hywel, Bishop of St. Asaph. His second wife was Gwenllian, a daughter of Rhys, prince of South Wales, and it is in connection with Gwenllian, that we have the pretty romance connected with the long absence from home, on one occasion, of Ednyfed, when he was either engaged in continental wars, or, more probably, as one of the Crusaders in the seventh and last Crusade, in which King Edward I. took a leading part. The romance is given in an old Welsh poem, entitled, "Ffarwel Edneved Fychain" (*Ednyfed Fychan's Farewell*), and the story runs thus :—Ednyfed left home on a warlike expedition, leaving his wife and children, in Llys Euryn. Before he started he sang a 'Song of Farewell' to his Gwenllian. Ednyfed was absent for so many years that he was given up as dead, and Gwenllian accepted the offer of a gentleman who had long sought her hand in marriage. On the night of the wedding, there came a beggar to the door of Llys Euryn, and on hearing the cause of the festivities that were going on, sought and obtained permission to go in and amuse the company. Asking for the old harp that used to be in the palace, he played various tunes, and finally the song, ' Ednyfed Fychan's Farewell,' and just as the wife and husband were leaving the place for their honeymoon, sang,

> Os bum ar ffo, dro yn druan—gwallus
> I'm golli Gwenllian !
> Ni chollaf—ewch chwi allan—
> Na gwely—na thy — na than !

(If I have been long a weary wanderer, and through my negligence have lost Gwenllian—yet will I have my own bed, my own house, my own fire ; so go ye hence !). Gwenllian recognising in the beggar her long-lost Ednyfed, forsakes the day's bridegroom and returns to Ednyfed.

The story is given in dramatic form in the short drama ' Ednyfed Fychan.'

PARISH CHURCH.

' Beautiful for situation ' is this substantial looking edifice, and it is built strongly on a rocky eminence, so as to resist the furious storms to which it is so exposed. The view from the churchyard is unsurpassed, and is a magnificent panorama of mountain, valley and sea. The Church was formerly the feudal chapel of Ednyfed Fychan, built under licence of the Pope ' for evermore to sing Divine Service,' and Ednyfed had authority to give his tithes and oblations to his chaplain there serving. The chapel probably stood in north side of the present north aisle, where are to be observed the filled-up arches. On the outside of the north wall the rugged edges of a wall stand out, suggesting a former extension, and the possible position of the chapel. Tradition says that there was an under-ground passage connecting Llys Euryn with the chapel. When the old parish church disappeared in the submergence of Morfa Rhiannedd, Ednyfed handed over his private chapel to the use of the parishioners of Dinerth. The Chapel was then enlarged, the result being the present north aisle. The south aisle was built by the Ladies Conwy, who also left a sum of money to repair and restore the present tower. The two aisles are separated by four arches of the late perpendicular period, and at their spring are carved stone angel-corbels. The two aisles thus make a building of the style of architecture adopted in the Clwydian Churches, examples of which you find at Whitchurch, near Denbigh, Abergele and others in the neighbourhood, the distinguishing features being a double nave, and no chancel. There are five windows, all filled with beautifully stained glass—the two in the East wall representing the Nativity and the Crucifixion—the two in the South wall representing the Resurrection and the Ascension, and that in the West wall, but recently built, representing

Lych Gate

St. Cecilia, the patron saint of music, David playing his harp, and Simeon singing the Nunc Dimittis.

In the north-west corner is a door leading to a vestry (constructed by the present Vicar, Rev. E. James Evans) and on to the tower, the top of which is reached by winding stone-steps.

On the south side of the Chancel is a *piscina*, a small stone basin into which the water used in the service of the Altar was poured, and which, as a rule, was connected with a drain pipe to carry off the water. In the east wall of the north aisle is an *ambry* or *almonry*, the place where alms used to be deposited, and which was also used as a receptacle for the sacred vessels of the Altar.

The *font* is an octagonal basin of Early English date, and has a beading of the nail-head ornament around the rim, and is quite perfect.

Standing in an upright position and fixed to the north wall of the Church is the coffin lid of the sarcophagus of Edny-fed Fychan. It was formerly near the Altar, where the re-mains of Ednyfed were placed when the Church was enlarged. The inscription in Saxon characters reads thus :—

Hic jacet Dns Edneved : Quodam Vicarius
Dedynert : Cs an propietur Deus. Amen.

(Vicarius means vicegerent, and Dedynert is the old name of the parish).

The memorial casket fixed over the entrance door is a modern construction, removed to its present position from the west wall, when the west window was made. It contains the ashes of a lady who died in 1893, and who was cremated.

The *tower* which is a massive and handsome structure, possesses some peculiar features such as loop lights with ogee heads, and with a stair in the South-west angle, over which rises a ' look-out ' or ' watch-place.' The structure of the tower and the absence of windows in the north wall, the oldest part of the Church, point out the various and many uses to which churches, built in districts where warfare was frequent, were put to. The church in such a district was so constructed that it often served not only as a place of worship or sanctuary, but also as a fortress in case of enemies' attack, and a look-out, whence to observe the approach of foes.

The battlements are stepped in the Irish fashion; the only church in North Wales besides this, that has stepped battlements, is Llanbeblig near Carnarvon.

The *Bell* bears the date 1752 and was cast by Ralph Ashton, Wigan.   Inscribed on it is

Edward Hughes }
William Evans } Churchwardens.
John Gwynn being Vicar.

CHURCHYARD.

The beautiful Churchyard is mostly of a rocky nature, and great difficulty is experienced in making graves, the rock having to be blasted by frequent small charges of powder. The depth of soil in the rocky part is very small, and in olden days graves must have been very shallow, for in 1909 when the paths were relaid, and various parts of the Churchyard beautified, bones were continually being dug up, and in some instances as, for example, under the slate-seat that used to be by the side of the porch, and where now, there is a rockery, whole skeletons were found.   In 1818 when lowering the Churchyard, a confused heap of bones were discovered, supposed to have been bones conveyed from the old churchyard just before it became submerged, and re-interred in the present one.   In 1907, when the foundations of the Lychgate were being strengthened, bones were dug up which lay under the surface of the road to Llandudno, showing how the Churchyard must have, at one time, extended over a greater area than its present one.

Near the spot where is now the main entrance gate there used to be an inn, known as the ' Ship.'   The large hawthorn-bush, still standing, rested on its roof.   The Inn was built in 1736, and taken down in 1874.

The *Sun-dial* which stands in a prominent position was given by Mary Jarvis of Dinerth in 1755.   The date 1712 on the base of the column seems to imply that this column was the base of a former sun-dial.   Under the bevelled edge is the inscription " Th. Owen, 1756."

The *Lych-gate* or Corpse-gate signifying the gate through which the dead body is borne on its way to burial, is one of the oldest in the district. It has the following inscription

Henry : Vaighan
Owen : Williams
Wardens.
Anno : Domini
1677.
M. R.

In 1677 the Vicar was Robert Foulkes, and the King was Charles II. M.R. are probably the initials of the builder, just as at the present day, you often find on a tablet built into the front wall of a house, the initials of the owner or builder, and the year in which the house was built. The suggestion that they stand for ' Mortui Resurgent ' (the dead shall rise again), while comforting, and not improbable, is rather fanciful.

ST. TRILLO.

This Saint, to whom the Church is dedicated, lived in the early part of the 6th century, and was one of the sons of Ithel Hael, who came with St. Cadfan, their kinsman, from Armorica to Wales, and became a member of the College of Bardsey. He was the brother of St. Tegai and St. Llechid. St. Trillo, together with St. Deiniol, Bishop of Bangor, and St. Crwst was among the signatories of the grant of certain rights by Maelgwyn Gwynedd to S. Kentigern, founder of the see of St. Asaph. The only two churches dedicated to or founded by St. Trillo are Llandrillo-yn-Rhos, and Llandrillo-yn-Edeyrnion in Merionethshire. In the north window of Llandderfel Church, which is situated between Llandrillo-yn-Edeyrnion and Bala, was *circa* 1699, a figure of " Sanctus Trillo Abbat." His day of commemoration—St. Trillo's Day—is June 15th, and it occurs in a great many of the early Welsh Calendars.

CAPEL TRILLO.

This ancient relic of the past, situated on the sea-shore, was built by Maelgwyn Gwynedd in the 6th century for St. Trillo, and is especially interesting as being a unique specimen of those oratories, which formed the type of the earliest British churches, and it corresponds to the primitive oratories

b

of Ireland and Cornwall. In form it is a parallelogram about
15 feet by 8 feet, the East end and both sides being pierced with
loop-holes, or lancets. The roof is vaulted and consists of
small stones. There is at the East end a perennial spring,
where, is is supposed, the first missionary baptised his converts,
and whence the water for Baptism in the several churches of
the parish in succeeding ages was religiously borne.

The existence of holy wells about Wales and the West of
England is a testimony of the way pagan ideas entered into the
religious beliefs of the common people, and tainted their
religious practices even with the consent of the clergy. Holy
wells, in fact, perpetuate the old heathen beliefs in the virtues
of running water, and when the country was converted to
Christianity, these wells were consecrated to some saint, the
Christians of the day probably defending the practice by saying
that the pool of Bethesda mentioned in the Gospel, was a holy
well. Reading the account of the Pool of Bethesda, and connecting with it the saying of St. James that ' the effectual
fervent prayer of the righteous availeth much,' it is not an
incredible thing to believe, that in the lifetime of a holy saint
such wells were capable of imparting beneficent qualities to all,
who in true faith approached and made use of them. However, time has the unfortunate tendency to cause abuses to
arise in connection with such old beliefs, and foolish practices
are apt to grow, such as those which have arisen in connection
with the well of St. Keyne in Somerset, that of St. Winifred in
Holywell, and that of St. Elian near Colwyn Bay. The latter,
for example, came to be used as a resort whither people,
wishing ill to their neighbours, went to curse them. No
superstitious practices are recorded as having been practised
at the Well of St. Trillo, and this fact may be regarded as in-
direct testimony to the purity and sincerity of the Saint that
has given it its name. It is not improbable that the little
oratory, or chapel of St. Trillo, was built for the purpose of
protecting the spring or well which exists at its east end.

There used to be formerly, another well associated with
the name of this saint, namely, " Ffynnon Trillo " (Trillo's
Well) in the parish of Llandrillo-yn-Edeyrnion.

RHOS FYNACH.

The religious zeal which characterised the 6th century and caused it to be known as the ' Age of the Saints,' was expressed amongst other ways, by the retirement into lonely places of some of the noblest sons of Wales to live as hermits. Eventually, many of them used to join together and live in retreats, making for themselves rules similar to those which governed the monasteries of later times. In the island of Priestholm, off the coast of Anglesey, then known as Ennislannach (Ynys Glanach) ' the ecclesaistical island,' and now known as Puffin Island, there dwelt hermits who supported themselves by the labour of their hands, and suffered no woman to approach their secure retreat. Bardsey, too, the ancient isle of saints, was thus taken possession of by saintly men, and early became inhabited by very religious monks called Coelibes or Colidei. There is no doubt that these Coelibes had many establishments all over Wales. Then arose the Latin monastic orders which obtained a footing in Wales in the time of the Normans. When the Cistercian Order took Europe by storm, the Welsh princes followed the prevailing fashion. and came forward as founders and benefactors of the new monasteries ; thus, in Wales we find that almost all the great monasteries were Cistercian.

When we remember that Capel Trillo is near Rhos Fynach, it is possible that there gathered around this oratory of St. Trillo a small community of saintly men, who made their dwelling in a hermitage on the site of the present Rhos Fynach. This hermitage may have been in existence when the Cistercians established themselves at Aberconwy, and that it was then annexed by the Cistercians and made a feu-farm subordinate to Aberconwy. This conjecture is supported by the fact recorded in history, that there was an old Celtic monastery at the foot of Snowdon, probably at Bedd-gelert, which had to fight for its very existence with the Cistercian monks of Aberconwy, who sought to annex it as a farm or subordinate cell, and with this view did their utmost to procure its destruction or to force its inhabitants to accept the rule of their order. I have given this conjecture in order to try and account for the way this district came into the possession of the Cistercian monks, for it is an established fact that Rhos Fynach—Rhos Monachorum, the Feu-farm of the monks—was an establishment subordinate to the Abbey of Aberconwy.

There is a charter dated 1230, which states that Prince Llewellyn owing to a quarrel with the Pope, alienated Rhos Fynach as a sign of his displeasure, and granted it to his marshal and Prime Minister Ednyfed. In this charter the church is referred to as the Church of Dineyrth, and the boundaries of the Rhos Fynach estate are given.

When Edward I. conquered Wales, he built the Castle of Conway, and afraid of the possibly hostile influence of a strong body of Welsh monks so near the Castle, destroyed the Abbey of Aberconwy.   He, however, did not deal harshly with the monks, for, with the consent of the Pope, he built them another Abbey, higher up the river Conway, at Maenan near Llanrwst.

At this time Ednyfed Fychan, grandson of the Ednyfed, mentioned above (see Framework of Cymric History, by Owen Rhoscomyl) seems to have restored Rhos Fynach to the monks of Maenan, and that it then became subordinate to Maenan. After the dissolution, the estate of Rhos Fynach passed into the hands of the Earl of Leicester, who held the lordship of Denbigh, and who in a charter dated June 30th, 17th of Elizabeth, granted it to Morgan ab John ab Dafydd of Maesewig, an ancestor of the late proprietor Thomas Lewis Parry Evans, by whom it was sold to its present owner.

In the drama ' Olwen of the Monk's Weir ' I have considered Rhos Fynach as a lesser monastery ; and though in the play, for obvious reasons, it is spared, it does not preclude the fact that, when the dissolution of the greater Monasteries took place in 1539, Rhos Fynach shared the fate of the Abbey of Maenan.

FISHING WEIR.

This interesting and historic feature in the parish is situated near Rhos Fynach and Capel Trillo, and is closely associated with both.   It is the only weir of its kind in Wales, and there are not many anywhere round the coasts of the British Isles.   This weir has been preserved owing to a Charter, a very ancient parchment, written in Monkish Latin, and signed ' Leycester,' the date of which is the 17th year of the Reign of Elizabeth, and which is now in the possession of the present owner of Rhos Fynach.

The Weir was built by the monks of Aberconwy about the year 1198. Its religious associations are confirmed by the fact, that the Bishop of the Diocese and the Vicar of the parish are entitled to the tithe of the fish caught in the Weir. Every tenth day from May 13th to October 18th, the fish caught in the Weir belong to the Bishop and the Vicar of the parish. From noon on Saturday until midnight on Sunday a law commands that the grating at the mouth of the Weir must be raised, so that no fish may be caught between those times. Prayers for the success and welfare of the Weir used to be made periodically at the shrine of St. Trillo close by, a custom observed at all the places on the sea-coast where tithes of fish were paid, and a custom which is still prevailing on the west coast of Ireland.

This Weir has been erroneously called in Welsh " Gored Wyddno " (*Gwyddno's Weir*) a mistake which has arisen through confounding it with the famous Weir of Gwyddno Garanhir (*Gwyddno with the high crown*) on which one night was entangled a leathern basket, containing a young child, who afterwards became the famous bard Taliesin. As this mistake is the cause of connecting the pretty romance of Taliesin with this weir, I make no apologies for introducing in a brief manner, this romance, especially as on it is founded the story of Olwen in the drama, ' Olwen of the Monks' Weir.'

Gwyddno Garanhir, the brother of Maelgwyn Gwynedd, was the lord of Cantref Gwaelod, a part of Cardiganshire and Merionethshire, which was submerged in the sixth century, owing to the carelessness of the drunken guardian of the dykes, named Saethynin. When Gwyddno saw the destruction that had fallen upon him, he is said to have broken out into the wild cry, resembling that of a Hebrew prophet.

" Stand forth, Saethynin, and behold the dwelling of heroes,
    —the plain of Gwyddno the ocean covers !
Accursed be the sea-guard, who after his carousal let loose
    the destroying fountain of the raging deep !
Accursed be the watcher, who after his drunken revelry
    loosed the fountains of the desolating sea !
A cry from the sea arises, even to heaven does it ascend,—
    after the fierce excess comes the long cessation !
A cry from the sea ascends above the ramparts,—

after the excess there ensues restraint !
A cry from the sea arises above the winds,—
after excess comes the far extending death ! ''

Gwyddno having thus lost most of his territory, had nothing
much to bequeath to his son Elphin, except the fishing weir,
which lay somewhere between Barmouth and Aberdovey.
Elphin, going one night to fish the weir, to his disgust found
nothing there excepting a leathern basket, entangled in the
stakes of the weir, and containing a baby-boy. Though he
could ill afford to support a foundling, Elphin, like a Christian,
took charge of the child and gave him a good education. The
boy, as soon as he came of age to understand all the kindness
that Elphin had shown him, sang

" Fair Elphin, cease to lament !
Never in Gwyddno's weir
Was there such good luck as that night.
In the day of trouble I shall be
Of more service to thee than three hundred salmon.''

The child became Taliesin (*radiant brow*), and was so named
when the leathern basket was opened, and the bright forehead
of a child was disclosed.

Many years after, Elphin paid a visit to his uncle Maelgwyn's court at Deganwy ; and, at a festival, feeling disgusted
and enraged at the proud boasting of his uncle's bards, and at
the fulsome compliments they paid to the king and his queen,
he spoke indiscreetly, saying ' of a truth none but a king may
vie with a king ; but, were he not a king, I would say that my
wife was as full of virtues as any lady in the kingdom, and also
that I have a bard who is more skilful than all the king's bards.'

His uncle, greatly incensed at Elphin's words, thrust him
into prison, vowing that there he would keep him until his
words were proved. Maelgwyn sent his handsome son Rhun
to encompass the corruption, by fair means or foul, of Elphin's
virtuous wife, but Taliesin upset, by a ruse, the vile scheme of
Rhun. Afterwards Taliesin went to Maelgwyn's court, and
challenged the king's thirty-three bards to a trial of skill,
saying in the course of the contest,

" If you be primary bards formed by heaven,
Tell your king what his fate will be.
It is I who am a diviner and a leading bard,

And will tell your king what will befall him.
A most strange creature will come from the sea-marsh of
　Rhiannedd,
As a punishment of iniquity on Maelgwyn Gwynedd.
His hair, his teeth, and his eyes as gold,
And this will bring destruction on Maelgwyn Gwynedd."

Taliesin then sang a wonderful song of the wind, the king declaring at its close that the boast of Elphin had been vindicated. Elphin was then set free, and Taliesin was promoted to high honour by Maelgwyn, who became his patron.

Taliesin afterwards became the chief bard of Arthur's Court, and he is said to have lived at one time by Lake Geirionydd, near Trefriw. He is supposed to have died about A.D. 570.

To the veneration paid him by his contemporaries, praise has been bestowed on him by each succeeding age, and by common voice, he is known as the ' Prince of the Bards.'

THE REV. E. JAMES EVANS.

THE STORY OF

EDNYFED FYCHAN

A Welsh Hero of the Twelfth Century.

DRAMATIS PERSONÆ.

EDNYFED	..	Prince, and General of 'Llewellyn the Great.'
HYWEL	..	Son of Ednyfed.
IORWERTH	..	Temporary Governor during Prince Ednyfed's absence
GWILYM	..	Confidential servant and Armour-bearer of the Prince.
MADOC	..	Boatman and Fisherman.
PEASANTS	..	Who bring the news of the devastation.
PRIEST	..	One of the Monks of Rhos Fynach.
MEGAN	..	Trusted old Nurse in the family.
MYFANWY	..	Daughter of Prince Ednyfed.
GWENLLIAN	..	Wife of Prince Ednyfed.
		Attendants and Guests.

ACT I.

SCENE. Old Llys Euryn : Early morning after an abnormal storm and tidal wave.

Enter Megan, *walking about disconsolately.*

MEGAN. I cannot understand it and am frightened. Twice last night did I hear the singing of the "teulu,"* once shortly after midnight then again with the dawning of the day, at the meeting of darkness and light. I have not heard them since the death of Cynan up Iorwerth. Twice in the same night ! This must portend something serious. What an awful storm was that last night ! It shook the rafters of this great house is if it meant to destroy it, and what a roar and raging of waters mingled with the blast ! But the "teulu !" what could they —— Oh heavens ! I forgot for the moment, the Prince went to meet the great Llewellyn

---

*Teulu means the spirits of departed relations who come back before some catastrophe or a death, and sing unseen.

yesterday at Carnarvon. What if he ——

[*Enter* Gwenllian *in great agitation.*

GWELLLIAN. Oh Megan! you here. Thank heaven for someone to converse with. All night have I kept vigil. What a terrible hurricane. Oh Megan, Megan, what if —— I cannot say it, my dread is choking me! what if —— thou knowest ——

MEGAN. Dear Lady, sit you down here: I know what is in your mind and tearing your heartstrings. Its the Prince, and he has not returned. The night was terribly stormy.

GWEN. I have an overwhelming fear upon me that some misfortune hath overtaken him. He kept me in perfect ignorance of his mission to Carnarvon yesterday, simply saying Gwilym would see to my wants and ——

[*Enter* Gwilym *in great haste, does not see* Gwenllian, *who is out of sight.*

GWILYM. Megan, my good woman, hast heard that —— (Gwenllian *comes forward*). I crave your pardon, my Mistress; for the moment I saw you not. But you look ill and anxious.

GWEN. What wonder, good Gwilym. Thy Master hath not returned—what and if the "Wylan" ("*Seagull*") hath been capsized in the gale! Good man, (*imploringly*) hast seen any signs of her?

GWILYM. No, my lady; I have been on the tower; she is not at the wharf. But be comforted, she sought shelter no doubt in the Menai, or perchance our Prince will bide the night at Tregarnedd.* I want not to frighten you, Lady, but the sea has——

[Peasants *rush in with the cry :*—

PEASANTS. Oh, Lady Gwenllian, the sea! the sea!

GWEN. (*excitedly.*) What of the sea, friends?

A PEASANT. Know you not, my Lady? It hath broken down the dykes again, as I knew it would one day. Maelor must have taken too much ale last night and left some of them open.

GWEN. Well, speak out, man, what has happened?

A PEASANT. The whole of Morfa Rhianedd is under water :

---

*Tregarnedd = the Prince's Estate in Anglesey.

the sea will not recede and the water is up to Capel Trillo*
and up to the rocks of Llysfaen.

GWEN.   Under water ! Then what of the sheep and cattle ?

ANOTHER PEASANT.   Nearly all drowned, my Lady, and
among them that drunken beast, Maelor, and serve him
right. We are ruined. But —— oh ! Lady ! I can scarcely
tell you ——

GWEN.   What ? What man ? Tell me the worst. Is my ---

ANOTHER PEASANT.   Some there are who have been drowned
in trying to save the cattle.

GWEN.   Who ? Speak someone. Quick !

ANOTHER PEASANT.   Rhys Llwyd of Rhyd Farm,† and two of
his men—the water rushed round, they could not escape.
Morfudd, Rhys' wife, is desperate ! Awful it is to see her
weeping. And, oh my Lady, our old Parish Church is gone
altogether, and most part of the Monks' weir.

MEGAN (*who has been listening intently*).   I felt sure some
calamity was at hand, for I heard the " teulu " singing
twice, and they are never wrong.

GWEN.   But where is my dear husband ? Where is Prince
Ednyfed ? Good people, waste not time : go and watch for
the boat and help her to land. Go at once, go ! (*Speaking
to* GWILYM). Stay, I want thee to carry a message to my old
serving-maid, Morfudd of Rhyd. She is in great sorrow.
Tell her my heart yearns for her —— perchance my own
good man lies in death also.

GWILYM.   Heaven forbid, Lady !

GWEN (*taking a purse out of her satchel*).   Give this to Morfudd
and tell her to keep it. It befits us to help one another in
times of sorrow. Poor girl, she has five children. See to it,
Gwilym.

GWILYM.   Yes, my good Mistress. I will go at once. (Megan
and Gwilym *exit together*.) (*Aside*). How kind she always
is !

GWEN (*left alone, sits down pensively*). (*Monologue*.) Yes, my
heart misgives me. 'Nyfed never told me what the urgent
business with Prince Llewellyn was. He has kept it this time

*Capel Trillo=the Oratory on the shore.
†Rhyd Farm=The Golf Links at Rhos.

to himself. It is important, I am sure. There has been for some time past something moody about him. He is more thoughtful and silent than usual. Gwynedd is now in one of its peaceful intervals. But who knows what new quarrel may suddenly be hatched! (*Rising and walking about*). We Welsh are so full of vengeance and battle, despite our warmness of heart. Ednyfed is of this temper : so is Prince Llewellyn. What do I know but that they have been planning some new expedition against the English, beyond Offa's Dyke. (*Walking in agitation*). Oh! would that this suspense was ended! I could nerve myself to receive the worst news if it must come, but this suspense is ——

[*Enter* Myfanwy *bursting in with skipping rope and* Hywel *with inflated bladder.*

MYFANWY. Father is coming up the road to the outer gate. (*Begins to skip*).

GWEN. Thank God!

MYF. He looks *so* wet and dirty as if he had fallen into the Conwy.

HYWEL. Father is coming along outside down there.

GWEN. God bless the lad for his good news.

[*Enter* Ednyfed *and* Madoc, *carrying a bag.*

EDNYFED (*walking with his strong and masterful stride*). Hallo, little wife, here I am at last. [*Seeing her agitation.*] But what ails thee dear one? Thou hast been crying, Gwenno! Eh?

GWEN. Yes, I have, indeed, for we all feared that the "Wylan" had foundered in the gale. You have been so long, 'Nyfed!

EDN. And no wonder, since Madoc and I had to walk nearly all the way from Penmaenmawr. The gale came on so suddenly. We were unprepared for it, and, had it not been for Madoc's skill and knowledge of seaway, I know not what would have become of us. It was just off that island where the birds nest, we call it Puffin Island, as thou knowest, the hurricane came on in its fury. Madoc put the snout of the "Wylan" straight to it. Then there came a fearful blast and a wave that hurled us well up to the moon, and I know not where besides. The mast snapped by the board, fortunately, or we would have been capsized. It was impossible to proceed. We got back somehow, I not know how, to Beaumaris, thanks to Madoc and the sailor lads under him, and managed to land under the shelter of a cliff.

[Madoc *exits.*

GWÉN. But how did you get home ?

EDN. I paid two seamen to row us across. Strong Madoc took an oar every other with each, and so we got across to Penmaenmawr with great difficulty, for the sea was still running high. I do not think anyone recognised Ednyfed in these draggled garments, until we came to Conwy city. There the ferryman, after some cautious scrutiny, did recognise me, and got four boatmen to row us to the wharf at Deganwy. But to tell the truth, once or twice I gave all up for lost. The hurricane was the worst I ever remember. What damage has it done in this direction ?

GWEN. Oh Ednyfed ! Something dreadful has happened ! The sea came in over Morfa Rhianedd* last night, breaking down the dykes, and has not returned. The Church is nowhere to be seen. The Weir is all but gone, and the sea has submerged the whole Morfa up to Llysfaen Rocks ! Probably much more damage has been done towards Abergele.

EDN. This is bad news ! Why should it have happened with such strong dykes ? I must go and investigate from yonder knoll. Having come back through the forest, I did not see the shore.

GWEN. There are at least three men drowned, not counting Maelor, poor Rhys of Rhyd and two of his men, in trying to save our cattle. And there may be more.

EDN. How knowest thou this, Gwen ? Who told thee ?

GWEN. Gwilym and the workmen.

EDN. Poor men ! Yea, and poor women and children too ! We must send help, Gwen.

GWEN. I have done that already in a small way. I sent Morfudd my purse this morning and all that was in it. But it was but little.

EDN. (*coming towards her and taking her two hands in his*). My good little Gwen ! always kind and thoughtful, and

---

*Morfa Rhianedd = a plain which once existed where now Colwyn Bay's blue waters entice the visitor.

wisely ready in emergencies ! Thou didst well. I must go
forth and try to do still more. Dost know where Madoc is ?
(*Calling loudly,*)   Madoc ! Madoc ! !

[*Enter* Megan, *hearing the Master's call.*

EDN. Where is Madoc ?

MEGAN. In the buttery, I think, my Lord.

EDN. Always in the buttery and kitchens ! By the bye, I
want thee to make me as many hose and legbands as thou
canst, with a cross in them, for I shall be in need of them
soon. Send Madoc hither forthwith.

[Madoc *enters somewhat crestfallen.*

EDN. Come, Madoc, my man ; we have something to do else
than fill our crops. I want thee forth with me to examine
into this devastation. Find Gwilym and bid him come also.
Let us all three see to it. (*Turning to* Gwen. *and waving
hand.*) I will not be long absent this time.   [*Exeunt.*

[*Enter* Iorwerth, *preceded by* Megan.

MEGAN. Sir Iorwerth, my Lady.

IORWERTH. I heard this morning of the great calamity that
has come upon you and your people on the Morfa, and have
come to offer my sympathy. Is his Highness the Prince
within the Palace ?

GWEN. I am sorry, Sir Iorwerth, he has gone forth to render
what help he can to these striken ones, and to see to the
burial of the unfortunate drowned. Sit you down, he will be
back ere long.

IOR. I see the sea hath broken down the dykes and taken free
possession of, I should say, the whole of Morfa Rhianedd,
even up to Abergele. This is a great loss of property, not to
mention sheep and cattle, and a considerable amount of
crops.

GWEN. It is indeed an alarming loss, but the loss of human
life is what troubles me most. Several of our faithful workmen were surrounded by the sea, in attempting to save the
animals, and were drowned.

IOR. But does not the Prince bethink him of his lost acres
more than the drowning of a few shepherds ? Why, he
must have lost miles of land along the coast.

GWEN. Of a truth he will miss his acres. But Enyfed hath a
good heart, and his first thought is for the widow and the

fatherless, and his dead workmen.

[Enter Ednyfed, *seeing* Iorwerth.

EDN.   Ha ! Sir Iorwerth, glad am I to see thee.   I pray thee
be seated.   I would have a word with thee later on upon a
matter of some importance.   This hath been a sad havoc.
I have just been to see to their burial.

IOR.   But what of thy lost lands ?

EDN.   Ah well, that is a loss, but I have not begun to think of
it as yet.   Wilt have some refreshment ?

IOR.   I thank thee, Prince, for thy ever ready offer of hospitality, but I must return to Conway without delay.   I came
but to show my sympathy.

EDN.   I thank thee, friend, and will accompany thee to the
outer gate.   [*Both exit.*

[Enter Megan *with the children.*

MEGAN.   Yes, dearie, it is a beautiful butterfly, you were
clever to catch it.   Do you remember the rhyme about the
life of a butterfly, Mistress Myfanwy ?

MYF.   Yes, my Megan, dear.
          " Who would be a butterfly,
              Born in a bower,   [*Enter* Ednyfed.
              Christened in a shower,
              Died in an hour ? "

EDN.   (*who has overheard*).   Well done, Myff, thou got'st the
flank side of old Megan that time.

HYWEL.   I can say a rhyme too, father.

END.   Bravo, my Hywel !   what is it, boy ?

HYWEL.   Come, Mary's feast,
              Come, Dewi's day,
              And then the little duck will lay.

                    (Ednyfed *takes him in his arms and
                        tosses him up above his head.*

EDN.   And thou art a duck too, my Hywel, a duck of a boy
and wilt do great things ere long, like my Prince Llewellyn.

MEGAN.   And like thy father too, my child, for though he does
not speak of his own deeds he is a rare brave man.

EDN.   There, there, Megan !   thou art my dear old nurse.   I
cannot remember thee as anything else but what thou art—
always good, always kind, always helpful.   And, by St.
Dewi, how thou didst play with me, and make me hang on

the apple tree branches to make my arms strong, as thou
puttedst it. There, little ones, go play.

[*Exit* Children.

MEGAN.   Yes, my Prince, and thy arms *are* strong. Oh would
those days were back again ! But I fear there is some trouble
before Prince Ednyfed. (Gwenllian *starts and listens*).

EDN.   Get along with thee, Megan ! Why, here I am safe on
dry land, and not an Englishman within Offa's Dyke.

MEGAN.   True, but I fear the trouble may be *beyond* Offa's
Dyke, or perchance *beyond the sea.*

EDN.   Set'st thyself off as a witch, Megan. (*In a bantering
way.*) I suppose I shall have to show thee my palm and
cover thine with silver. Tut ! Tut ! do not talk foolishness,
good woman.

MEGAN.   It is not foolishness, my Master, but anxiety.   I
heard the warning twice last night.

GWEN (*rising and coming forward*).   Heard it ! Heard what ?

MEGAN.   The " teulu " ! I heard the hymn quite plainly
twice over.

EDN.   Get along with thee, Megan ; thou art getting old and
imaginative ! Thou ——

GWEN.   Be patient, 'Nyfed, let her tell us what she heard.

MEGAN.   I heard quite plainly, just behind the Llys, the hymn
we often sing in the Prince's private Chapel on the hill
yonder. " Ave ! ave ! "   Listen, I hear it now, in daylight !
How awful ! (*All listen.   Hidden choir sings*).

" Ave ! ave ! Forwyn fwynaf,
        At yr allor 'r ym yn dwyn
Cyrph y meirw, O Fendicaf,
        Gyda phader Iesu mwyn,
Dyma'r crair sydd holl fendigaid,
        Sef y Groes, y Dwyfol Bren ;
O er mwyn yr Oen aberthwyd,
        Gad i'n gwrdd tu draw i'r llen."

My good Master, whom I nursed as a child, did you hear
that ? Do not go away ! the " teulu " warneth you.

EDN.   I heard nothing. Did'st thou, Gwen ?

GWEN.   No, I cannot say I did.

EDN.   Away with this superstitious nonsense ! Come along,
come into the garden, Gwen, and let us have a walk before

the darkness sets in. [*Exeunt.*

MEGAN (*lingering behind*). Something important will happen !
[*Exits.*

END OF ACT I.

ACT II.

SAME SCENE. Three days later.

Enter Children *with their toys.*

HYWEL. Come, Myfanwy, wilt thou have a game of soldiers ?

MYF. Oh yes, brother mine, I love soldiers ; they are so brave !
Art going to be a soldier, Hywel ?

HYWEL. Yes, I want to be a great warrior like father and
grandfather, Marchud ap Cynan, and cut off the heads of the
English, as father does. (*Having placed the pegs in the
ground*). Now then, look out (*Throws clubs at* Myfanwy's
pegs). You are the *English*, and I am the *Welsh*. There they
go ! (*When pegs are knocked down*).

MYF. (*failing*). Oh, that slipped ! Wilt give me another try ?

EDN. (*entering quietly with* GWEN, *amused*). Well, my young
combatants, what are ye playing at ? Eh ?

HYWEL. Oh father, it is a big battle between the Welsh and
the Saxons. I am the Welsh and she (*pointing*) is the Saxons.
I have killed three of her champions ; but she has not killed
one of mine.

EDN. (*entering into the fun*). I take Myf's side. (*Throws club*).
There they go ! Champions or no champions. (*Shrieks of
delight from* Myf.)

GWILYM (*entering and grimly amused*). My Prince ! There are
many cattle drowned, but worse than that, corpses of
drowned men have been washed up on the shore by the in-
coming tide. They are strangers to us. There is one
foreigner, and this is a ring we found on one of his fingers.
[*Exit* Children.

EDN. Honest Gwilym ! Honest and modest as ever thou
wast ! Let's see it, man. (*Examining ring*). Why, this is
of Eastern workmanship, I trow, and likely to be valuable.
Gwen, my cariad, look at this——a rare and beautiful gem !

c

Gwen, I will leave this in thy keeping. It is a present from
the sea, and I would give it thee.   [*Exit* Gwilym.

GWEN. I muchly thank thee, 'Nyfed. How ever ready art
thou, my Prince, and husband. to bestow gifts on thy Gwen.

EDN. (*taking her hands fondly*). Thou should'st have said thy
beautiful Gwen, for the whole of Morganwg was in raptures
over thy beauty till I came and brought thee here as my
bride, my pretty one. But thou always wast modest and
discreet, and I love thee better for those sweet qualities.

GWEN. Thou art too flattering, 'Nyfed, and dost spoil me
daily. What of those poor drowned folk ?

EDN. Ah ! yes, how thoughtless of me to forget them for the
moment in thinking more of *thee !* (*shouting*) Madoc ! Madoc !
[*Enter* Madoc]. Madoc, my man, come with me, and let as
see to the burial of these poor drowned men. Stay, bid
Gwilym come also.   [Madoc *exits, also* Ednyfed.

MEGAN (*entering alone*). You seem sad, my lady.

GWEN. Yes, Megan, I feel lonely and unhappy. I feel as if
something momentous is about to happen. Thy hearing
" the teulu " has unnerved me. There is something mysterious all around us---the sea, the storm---my husband's silence
---all frightens me. I am not usually easily scared ?

MEGAN. No, my Mistress, you are ever the bravest of brave
women (*warmly*).

GWEN. Look at this ring. It was found on the hand of a
drowned foreigner on the shore. There is something strange
about it. The Prince has given it to me.

MEGAN (*examining the ring*). It has a curious glitter, which I
have never seen before. It seems as if there was a smouldering of fire within. Methinks that it bears with it either good
or evil, and that, may be, it will prove to be a link in the chain
of my Lady's life !

GWEN. How fraught with superstition thou art, Megan.
Thou seest something ominous in every flutter of a bird or
movement of an animal.

MEGAN. There are things we cannot ken, which are partly
revealed to us for our warning, my lady. The spirit of the
dead are all around us. I hear them singing and speaking.

GWEN. What, now ?

MEGAN. No, but at times, night and day. I hear nothing now.

Still I have heard the "teulu" several times a few days gone by. Harken! my Mistress! What is that? (*Singing of hidden Choir*).

EDN. (*Entering*). Why, Gwen, you look scared! What troubleth you?

GWEN. The sound of singing far away. (*Excitedly*).

EDN. Fear not, dear one. It is but the bearing of the drowned to their burial. Now are they on their way to the place of burial, and are singing the usual old hymns. I will warrant me, Megan has been croaking again like the old *Bryn Euryn ravens. [*Exit* Megan.

GWEN. We have had somewhat melancholy conversation, and I feel something sombre creeping over me. Hast discovered aught of that foreigner whose ring thou gavest me?

EDN. Nothing. He is evidently from an Eastern land. But there is nothing to denote from where . . . . . Now, Gwen (*leading her to a seat*), wilt listen to me earnestly for a little? I have something important to communicate to my dearest one.

GWEN. (*Startled, looking him straight in the face*). What? Tell me, 'Nyfed, tell me at once. I have felt for days that something passing strange was going to happen. Tell me at once! and end this horror of suspense.

EDN. Dear little Gwen, I am going to leave thee again for a while, by permission of my Prince Llewellyn.

GWEN. Keep me not in this agony of ignorance. Where art thou going? To the Marches?

EDN. No, fair one, a bit further. I am going to seek new laurels and renown to ——

GWEN. Where, for God's sake?

EDN. It is for God's sake. It is to the *Holy Land*.

GWEN. What! With the crusaders?

EDN. Yes, with the crusaders. My mind is set upon it. I feel I *must* go. It is a great matter. Something urges me to go, with a stout heart and a strong arm, to wrest my Saviour's Tomb from the desecrating hand of the heathen. (*Gwenllian breaks down*). Come, Gwen, weep not; don't; Gwen, don't! Thou hast ever been my brave lady; do not away with thy

---

* Bryn Euryn = the hill above the ruins.

gallantry to-day.

EDN.   Forgive me, 'Nyfed, forgive me! I cannot help it.   I
have a horrible dread that I shall never see thee again if thou
goest forth.

EDN.   It is a good cause! and, trusting as I do in the Ever-
lasting Arms, yes, " He who covers our heads in the day of
battle," I am sure thou'lt see me back again ere long.   Now
I must forth to prepare, for we go *to-night*.

GWEN.   (*Astonished*).   To-night!

EDN.   Yes, beloved; I have kept this departure from thy ken
as long as I could, so as to save thee from fretting.

GWEN.   But thou could'st not; I have been fretting for days,
not knowing thy intention.

EDN.   I knew not of that; take heart, Gwen.   All will work
out to my honour.   Here cometh Gwilym for to make ready.
Well, my faithful Gwilym, hast all ready now?   [Gwilym

GWILYM.   Not all, my Master, but most.   *entering*.

EDN.   Thou art ever careful and ready.   We are away to-night
on a long and eventful journey.   Hast thou a strong heart to
set forth with?

GWILYM.   Good Master, you will not find Gwilym wanting
when anything of danger comes.   I am but a poor creature
when at my best ——

EDN.   No, no; twice hast thou saved my life.

GWILYM (*continuing*).   I am poor at my best, but your server
Gwilym will die for you, my noble Prince, if need there is.
Who would not be proud to follow a warrior who cut off the
heads of three of the English champions, and has them now
as his coat of arms?   If I mistake not, we shall have more
to add to them ere we return.

EDN.   Stop, stop, my good Gwilym! to hear thee speak I
might be a Samson or Judas Maccabeus; but, as I am
neither, thou art wasting thy intellect and oratory.   But
who comes here?   [*Enter* Priest *and* Peasants

PRIEST.   May it be our good fortune to have a short audience
with thee?   We are in dire distress.   It must be known to
thee, ere now, that the sea hath robbed us of our sacred
Sanctuary.   Besides the loss of a vast amount of cattle and
property, God's House itself has been destroyed.   What are
we to do?   Conway Priory is afar off, and the small Oratory

at Rhos Fynach, besides being too small, hardly becomes the
dignity of a Parish Church. Our brother Monks in Rhos
Fynach are hard pressed in mind to know how to provide for
the spiritual requirements of the people. Canst thou, our
honoured Prince, help us out of our difficulty ?

EDN. What wouldst thou, father, for I can see thou hast a
something smouldering in thy active brain ? Speak out,
good father, and you, my honoured neighbours. Unfold
your thoughts. What is it ?

PRIEST. With trepidation, our Lord Prince, we have come to
ask you, saving your Princely presence, if the parishioners of
Dinerth may be permitted to enter your Feudal Chapel on
the hill, to offer our daily devotions to the Omnipotent ?
Elsewhere we have no appropriate or consecrated building.

EDN. Good father, I have something to tell thee. I have
made a vow to go forth, with many more, to the Holy Land
to wrest our Saviour's Tomb from the hand of the heathen.
It may, perchance, be my lot never again t o see Llys Euryn,
and never again to bend the knee in that chapel yonder. I
have also been saved from shipwreck ! Considering, therefore, our people's sacred deprivation and the demolishment
of our Church, I now and for ever make over my private
Chapel on the hill to your use. Yes, let it be yours, friends
and neighbours, as well as the tithes and oblations, till the
end of time. In confirmation of this, my promise to you,
I hold up my hand in the presence of the Triune God.

PRIEST. Noble Prince ! Nobly done ! Nobly spoken ! Methinks that an investment has here been made to-day, the
just and sacred interest of which will not be inconsiderable
when the books are opened at the final *balancing*. We heart-
fully thank thee.

EDN. I thank *thee*, father, for thy kind words. Give me thy
blessing ere we part—perhaps for ever in this life.

PRIEST. (*Raising hand in benediction*). The Lord be with thee,
and keep thee in safety, and prosper thee in the day of battle,
and give thee the victory, and return thee to thy house and
people in His own good time.

EDN. Amen. . . . Fare-thee-well, father ! Have a kind care
for my Lady Gwen, when I am absent. See that no harm
comes to her. Fare-thee-well.

[*Exit* Priest *and* Neighbours.

> [Gwilym *stumbles in with baggage.*

Hast thou all in readiness now ? Do not forget the special
sword, and that coat of mail I wear beneath, thou knowest ?–
GWILYM. All this is ready, my Prince.

> [*Enter* Gwenllian *and* Children.

Gwilym, my man, we would be alone ! Seest thou ?
GWILYM. I see, my Master, I have something to do for myself
by way of preparation, but will be within call if my Prince
needs me.   [*Exits.*
EDN. (Gwen *and* Children *alone with him*). Now, my dearest
one, my fair Gwen, we must say good-bye. 'Tis hard, but
we have done so before.
GWEN. How long wilt thou be absent ? (*Bravely*).
EDN. I know not, my sweet one ; it may be for years. But,
Gwen, thou wilt not forget me ? I will not forget thee !
Think on me daily—nightly ! When the bright stars shine
above, say in thy heart :—" I remember and love 'Nyfed " ;
and I will say in my heart :—" I remember and love my
Gwen." Let the stars be a talismanic link between thee and
me, however far from one another we may be.
GWEN. They shall, my noble and dear husband. Thou mayest
be well assured I will not forget.
EDN. Now, Gwenno, I am going to sing thee a song, which I
have composed on purpose for this hour. I dedicate it to
thee, dear one, and let it be called, if thou wilt, " The Farewell of Ednyfed."

SONG.

i.

" The call has come from beyond the main,
" Brief our parting, if long our pain,
" Silent the harp-string when sorrow is sorest,
" Blithely we'll sing when we meet again ;
" God, He wills it ! Flash bright my sword
" Fierce and strong is the Paynim horde
" Who but a coward would tarry at home
" When infidels hold the home of his Lord."

ii.

" The salmon he knows his path in the sea,
" The twint he returns to his own oak-tree,

" The curlew seeketh the same crag-side,
" But who can tell where my path shall be ?
" God, He wills it ! Away ! Away !
" Be it death to go, it were shame to say :
" Death is the seal of lover's true loving,
" Shame were death to our love for aye."

iii.

" Fret not for what is beyond recall,
" Fear not whatsoever befall,
" Fear is for cowards and comes of the devil,
" Death is God's mercy, lighting on all ;
" God, He wills it ! Farewell my son,
" Guard thine honour as I have done ;
" Farewell, my Gwenllian, my life, my heart's treasure,
" Though waters divide us, in love we are one ! "

[Gwenllian *listens, first sadly, then at last
breaks down completely.*

EDN. Keep it in thy mind, my Gwen. (*Turning to the* Children
who look in wonder). Come here, my little ones. Ye know
not what a " Crusade " means. I am going away for, perhaps, a long time (*kneeling down with an arm round both*) to
fight for Jesus Christ's sake in the land in which He lived and
was slain and was buried ; but thou knowest Hywel, what
happened three days afterwards ?

HYWEL. He came alive again.

EDN. Yes, my boy ; but there are some evil minded people
who say he did not. I am going to join others many, who
are going to rescue the grave in the rock and keep it, if we
can, in Christian hands. Understandest thou this ?

HYWEL. Yes, father, I think I do. Thou art going away to
fight for Christ. I wish I was big enough to come with thee.

EDN. Well said my son ! Perhaps the day may come. When
I am away on fields of battle do you fight *peacefully* at home.
Fight in your heart against all that is evil. Obey your
Mother, and have a care to do all that is brave and honour-
able. (*He kisses them, lays his hands on their heads, and
turning, standing to* Gwenllian). Fare thee well ! Sweetest
and dearest. It is useless to utter words ! Thou wast ever
brave, when I went forth to the Marches ! Thou wilt be

brave again to-day. I have made all arrangements for
Tregarnedd and Clwyd's estates as well as for Llys Euryn.
Sir Iorwerth of Conwy, my old play-mate and comrade in
arms, will see to all. Fear not, my Cariad, and heaven protect thee! (*Embracing her*). Fare thee well! [*Exits.*
                                (*Sounds of horns and shouting.*

GWEN. (*at the door calls him back*). Ednyfed, thou gavest me
that strange ring. Take it with thee and, please God, bring
it back again.

EDN. I think I see thy meaning. I feel a strength in thy
prayer. Please God I will come back again !
                                [*Embraces and exits as before.*

MEGAN (*entering quietly*). My dear, dear Lady, my heart bleeds
with thine. I pray thee come to thy chamber.   [*Exeunt.*

END OF ACT II.

ACT III.

SCENE.   The same as before.
TIME.   Six years later.

GWENLLIAN *sitting by spinning wheel and
meditating in monologue.*

GWEN. More than six years since our parting ! Oh Ednyfed,
my dear Prince, how long thou hast been absent! Wilt
thou ever return ? I wish I could hear the " teulu " like
old Megan. It is passing strange. Many of the Crusaders
have returned, and yet my Ednyfed, the brave man of my
heart, lingers long in coming. Despondency creepeth over
me—a cold shudder. What and if he is slain ! I fear me he
is among the gallant dead. Gwilym, too, hath not returned.
That adds to my fears. Father Dewi hath given up hope,
though the good man counsels patience. Iorwerth is without
hope and does not endeavour to hide his hopelessness.
Iorwerth has been kind and good, and honest, and done my
every behest. The estates have been well looked after under
his excellent management, especially Tregarnedd. The
flocks and the forests ——

MADOC (*entering with cap in hand*). My Lady, Sir Iorwerth of

Conwy, coming from Anglesea, craveth audience.

GWEN. (*aside.*) How strange that I was thinking of him just then. Bid him enter, Madoc. Stay, hast caught any fish this morning ? My faithful friend Sir Iorwerth will probably dine with me this day.

MADOC. Yes, my Mistress, I caught a fine salmon this morning, and a few other fish of small account over night. They are in the larder.

GWEN. That is well. Bid the kitchen woman serve a good meal at noon. [*Exit* Madoc.

MADOC. Yes, Lady. (*Aside.*) I have suspicions.

IOR. (*ushered in by* Madoc). Good day to thee, lady. Here is thy humble servant come to inflict himself upon thee again.

GWEN. Use not the word inflict. Glad am I to see thee at all times (*earnestly*). Thou art my faithful friend. Hast any news from Palestine ?

IOR. No, my dear Patroness, I fear the worst, in truth I do. All agree with me in my fears. Nearly *seven* years has he, my old playmate and fellow-in-arms, been away and nothing heard of him from those who have returned. After the last battle he seems to have disappeared.

GWEN. Think'st thou he hath died in battle ?

IOR. Gwenllian—(*correcting himself*). I crave pardon—*Lady* Gwenllian. It——

GWEN. (*interrupting*). Benig such an old and valued friend thou canst call me Gwenllian, apart from *Lady*.

IOR. Then call me plain Iorwerth, for I would have it so by preference.

GWEN. I thank thee friend : then be it so Iorwerth (*accentuated*). I know not what I should have done without thee. Thou hast been right-hand and oracle in true earnest to me in my husband's absence.

IOR. Gwenllian, it hath been a work of pleasure, may I add a labour of *love ?* (Gwen. *pleased, but rather uncertain of I.'s meaning.*)

MEGAN (*entering at an awkward moment*). I pray you, my Lady, I cannot find the children. Know you where they may chance to be ?

GWEN (*rather confused*). I have sent them to gather flowers for me in the Dinerth meadows. See to the supply in the

Ruins of Llys Euryn.

buttery. Sir Iorwerth dines with me this day.

MEGAN (*aside.*) I like not the look of things. There is mischief in that man's eyes. [*Exits.*

IOR. Gwenllian, I have not been without fearing that thy heroic lord will not return to thee again. Shouldst thou not have a strong arm and a loving heart beside thee—*always* beside thee—to guard thee, for there is no denying that the times are troublous ?

GWEN. I grasp not quite thy meaning. Dost suggest that I should enter into the bonds of wedlock once again ?

IOR. Yes, dear Gwenllian, that is what my mind now runs upon. Why not ? Thou knowest that, after seven years, the wife of a crusader is regarded as a widow.

GWEN. Good friend, no one, so far, has sought my hand ; and as long as I have thee to look after my interests, I am sure all will be for the best.

IOR (*with much emphasis*). Thou *couldst* rely *always*, my dear Gwen, thou knowest it ! (*Sitting beside her and taking her hand*).

GWEN (*considerably confused*). Couldst didst thou say ? *Canst* should have been the word.

IOR (*passionately*). "Canst" or "couldst" it matters not, I cannot keep it from thee any longer. I have—I have something to tell thee, something to give thee. Ever have I admired thee. In truth I *loved* thee secretly. Give to me, Gwen, that one sweet privilege, the one hope of my life ; give to *me* the privilege of protecting thee always—the privilege of calling thee my own, my very own beautiful Gwen. Always have I envied Ednyfed the possession of the fair gem which shines in Llys Euryn. Do, Gwen, my beloved do ! !

GWEN (*greatly perturbed*). How can I, how *can* I, not knowing whether Ednyfed is dead or alive ?

IOR. He *must* be dead, and the seven years are now completed.

GWEN. No, not completed. There are three more months to run.

IOR. But thou dost not say me nay. Come, my pretty one, promise me, if I wait for thee these long, lingering three months, that thou wilt wed me !

GWEN. Iorwerth, I will speak now my inmost feeling in respect

of thee. I have, by my trust and dependence in and on thee,
learnt to do something more than respect thee. I cannot say
I love thee quite, for I loved Ednyfed so dearly. Never can I
love another as I loved him. (*Rising much overcome*). Wait
for the three months to elapse, and then ——

IOR.   What then ?

GWEN.   I will tell thee the conclusion I have come to.   For the
present, fare-thee-well !

        (*He kisses her hand, both exit opposite directions.*

CHILDREN (*entering with* MEGAN).   Mother ! Mother !

GWEN (*from above*).   Yes, dear ones, here I am.

        [*They exit with her.*

MEGAN.   Much would I give to know what passed between that
man and my lady.   He hath designs upon her, and, if I
mistake not, not forgetful of the property.   Oh would that
the Prince would return.

MADOC (*entering*).   Hallo ! old Meg, unpacking thy box of
memories as usual.   Thy face looks long and lengthening !
Hast seen or heard or smelt anything this morn ?   Thou
should'st start a sweetheart Meg.

MEGAN (*with disdain*).   Sweetheart forsooth !   Me thinks there
is too much of that already within these walls.

MADOC.   But sweets *are* sweets, and there can be none too
much of them.   (*Coming towards her*).   Look here now——

MEGAN (*interrupting him.*)   Out with thee, dunderhead, thee
and thy sweets !   'Twould take much to sweeten thee.   Thy
very face is as sour looking as a posset of buttermilk and
vinegar !

MADOC.   Come, come ! old playmate !   Don't disparage me
nor thyself.   Thou lookest as young to-day as thou didst
forty years gone by.   By the saint's thou doest ! (*laughing*).

MEGAN (*exasperated*).   Forty years said'st thou, why I am
barely forty now and——

MADOC (*interrupting*).   Never mind, sweetheart ; we two ran a
helter-skelter childhood together in the Gloddaeth woods,
and I know I am nearer sixty than forty, and though a few
years younger thou art also if ——

MEGAN.   (*Picking up a stick, makes for him*).   I'll teach thee to
behave thyself (*chases him about*).

MADOC (*in roars of laughter*).   Ah ! wouldst thou?   (*dodges*).

How sweet are women's ways (*dodges again*). Hai! that
was near my *corin*! (*stumbles on hands and knees.* Megan
delivers blow). Oh, oh.

MEGAN. There, that's sweets for thee, thou mule! (*sits down
exhausted*).

GWEN (*coming down*). Methought I heard a sound of wrangling
What! Megan! Madoc!! What meaneth this?

MADOC (*still panting*). I crave your pardon, my Lady, but we
were discussing the difference between sweets and buttermilk, and somehow we couldn't quite agree in our argument
or, or, er—come to a final conclusion.

MEGAN (*recovered and standing*) Methinks I did my Mistress,
and what is more I believe, I made an impression!

MADOC (*aside.*) Heavens! she did! (*rubbing his back*).

GWEN (*to* Madoc). 'Twere better for thee to go mind thine
own business. Much there is to do if thou would'st but do
it!

MADOC. I obey, my Lady.   [*Exit*

GWEN. (*Turning to* Megan). What meaneth this legend of
sweets and buttermilk? It soundeth strange. Say on.

MEGAN (*in difficulty*). It was only a passing quip, my Lady,
and not worth paying heed to.

GWEN. I could not fail but hear thy angry words and something more in my descent from chamber. There must be no
disorder here, now our Prince be absent; besides Iorwerth
the faithful, cannot be always present to keep ye in order.

MEGAN (*aside*). He is far too present. (*Aloud.*) Do not trust
that man, my dear Mistress!

GWEN. My good woman, what possesseth thee? Never a
more faithful man treadeth earth.

MEGAN. Lady Gwenllian, I fear I presume greatly, still, on
account of the love I have for my Lady and her noble Lord,
I will venture to say that you are mistaken in his fidelity,
and that this Iorwerth is not worthy of touching your shoe-
buckle. O, I pray you——

GWEN (*interrupting angrily*). Megan, desist! How darest
thou thus to speak to the Lady Gwenllian!

MEGAN (*earnestly pleading*). If it please you——

GWEN (*very angrily*). Thou had'st better betake thy impertin-
ent self to the children's playground. Thou art in thy
second childhood!

MEGAN. Before I go, in all sincerity—I am an old servant in this great family—in all humility, I take this advantage of mine age to say to my mistress : —Listen not to the serpent wiles of the designing Iorwerth. He is a cunning and a bad man. Be true to your Lord, my Lady ; he may yet return. List not to——

GWEN (*in great anger*). Megan, have I not commanded thee to go ?

MEGAN. Yes, my Mistress.

GWEN. Then go ! !——When I want thy advice, I will ask for it.   [Megan *exits.*

(Gwen, *alone*)——I am distraught. My mind like cross currents flows unevenly. My husband ! is he dead ? Iorwerth says so : Father Dewi fears so : and so do I——(*pause*). Sir Iorwerth seeketh my hand—(*pause*). He has been good, and is of goodly appearance. But still something hindereth my yielding to him, and now Megan hath spoken sinister words of him which have thrown my mind into a turmoil. What am I to do ? (*pause*). Darkness ! (*pause*). O for some light ! (*Suddenly*) *standing as she exits to bed-chamber*). It becometh me to think much of this, ere my decision is made.

MEGAN (*appearing quietly*). She has retired. I must seek her forgiveness, for I spoke as I should not have done.

END OF ACT III.

ACT IV.

SCENE. The same as before.

TIME. After the three months have elapsed.

MADOC (*entering*). May the saints be blessed for such a " neithior "* as this. The gifts are many and costly. My lady Gwenllian has to thank her pretty face and ankles neat for many a splendid gift. " Catto pawb "†! did not the " medd " ‡ flow ? There is but one thing wanted—a harp.

---

*" Neithior " means a sort of Welsh reception of neighbours before or after the wedding. Gifts were given to bride and bridegroom. This custom still survives in Cardiganshire.

†" Catto pawb ! " an ejaculation. Keeps us all !

‡" Medd," a sort of drink made of the honeycomb.

Unfortunate it is that old Caradog is bound in his bed with rheumatics. Still they are making the best of it yonder. (*Hidden choir singing* " *Hob y deri dando* ") just hear them ! (*joins in the chorus lustily*].

MYF. (*rushes in excitedly*). Madoc, my friend, is Megan here ?

MADOC. Am I old Megan's keeper ?

MYF. Somehow, of late I find thee and my dear Megan much in the same place (*quite innocently*).

MADOC (*amused*). No, my little sunbeam, she is not here. (*Disdainfully*). Probably, she is larking in the culinary department ! Old Meg knows what's good, and to-day good is at its best !

MYF. And thou knowest what's good, or my eyes deceive me greatly this day. (*Drawing near, lowering voice*). Is it true what Megan says, that we are going to have another father ?

MADOC (*aside*). What a lobsided hulk Megan is ! Her jib and mainsail flop about, and she wobbles with a capful of wind ! (*to* Myf.) By the spirit of cookery here she cometh from the culinary department, as I expected. (*Aside*). Now I must have some fun ! (*Singing outside,* " *Ar hyd y Nos.*") (*To* Megan). Well, my friend of long years gone by, and going by far too fast, what thinkest thou of this great " neithior " ?

MEGAN. I think little of it ; it leadeth to no good. (*Aside*). How I hate that evil Iorwerth ! (*To* Myf.) Come with me, my dear one, thy mother wanteth thee in the garden.

MADOC (*mockingly*). Take no more " medd," old sweetheart, lest it prove to thee too strong a breeze with thy want of ballast.

MEGAN. Hold thy tongue, thou jellyfish, and go and cool thy fishy head in the weir. [*Exit* Megan *and* Myf.

MADOC. How merrily they are singing. (*Un, dau, tri, phedwar, pump, chwech, &c., ;* Madoc *hums the refrain and says*) : I cannot refrain further from the feast, though the codfish even know I have had quite enough already. What did she call me ? A jellyfish ! Well, a jellyfish hath an open mouth and it seemeth meet for me, according to dear old crusty Meg, to open mine, if I can but find the wherewith to fill it.

[*Proceeds to exit ; meets* VAGRANT
tattered and torn.

Hallo, old scarecrow, whence comest thou ? 'Twas but
yester-e'en I planted thee in Bryn Defaid field. Hast un-
planted thyself and returned so soon ?

VAGRANT. Hold thy garrulous tongue in check, friend, and
tell me, prithee, what this merry-making in this old and
princely hall ? I see thou hast not gone without wherewith
to make thee merry, whereas others like myself have. What
revel proceedeth here ?

MADOC. It is the Lady Gwenllian's " neithior," an thou must
know. To-morrow she weds the noble Iorwerth of Conwy.

VAGRANT. Then there is open house this day ? Could I
break my fast beneath this hospitable roof ?

MADOC. It would seem that everybody is welcome, even such
as thee ! But thou art more like to scare the company than
please them.

MEGAN (*entering*). Who have we here, Madoc ? One of thy
boon companions, witless as thyself ? Thou art wanted,
lazy ! (*pointing to exit*).

VAGRANT (*after* Madoc *exits*). Good woman, I hear the sound
of revelry and would take part therein, if but admitted. I
am short of befitting apparel ; canst find me change of
garments ?

MEGAN. Thy words seem to me not in keeping with thy
garments. What makes it move my mind to think that I
have seen thee here before ? Art thou a wandering minstrel
fallen on evil days and perchance on evil ways ?

VAGRANT. I have done a little in the way of minstrelsy, and
it is probable that thou hast seen me before. I have, as
thou said'st fallen upon evil days—just look at me.

MEGAN. (*Looking him up and down, fastens her eyes an his
stockings, looks him in the face and says*). My Prince Ednyfed ! I know you now, however greatly altered.

EDN. Why sayest thou this with such confidence ? Do I look
Princelike ? Thou art imaginative, friend !

MEGAN (*pointing to the tattered stockings*). Those I knit with
these my own hands, e're my Prince went forth, and I know
them by the sign of the cross I knitted into them. And to
prove it still further, pardon me, my master (*opening his
shirt*) here I find on the right shoulder the scar of that wound
you received at the battle of Castell Crogen on the Marches.
You are Ednyfed. (*Takes his hand and kisses it reverently
and fervently*).

EDN. Megan, my dear old nurse, thou hast found me out.
True and faithful as ever hast thou been to me and mine.
This is a strange home-coming ! By a strange chance, I,
Ednyfed, arrive at my own doorstep on the very eve of my
wife's second marriage, and that with him, whom I called
and thought my friend. We shall have a word to say of this
later on to-night. Get me some apparel wherewith to dis-
guise myself. Tell this to no one, but let me in unto the
revelry as a wandering minstrel. [*Both exit.*
[*Here enter guests as many as possible, preceded by*
Gwenllian *and* Iorwerth.
IOR. (*To* Gwen. *aside*). Ah, my pretty one, this has been a
joyful day, and to-morrow thou wilt be mine, yes, Gwen, my
very own ! my star, my Queen !
GWEN. (*aside*). I thank thee, Iorwerth, for thy loving words.
I see that thou lovest me, and I love thee, but not quite as I
loved my lost Ednyfed. Canst not expect that ? (*Aloud*).
Let us have music and dancing. Alas ! I forgot, Caradoc is
ill, and cannot take his accustomed place. There can be no
harp, nor harper to-night. (*Aside*). There seems to be a
gloom falling on all.
THE MINSTREL (*in the far back*). I once could do a little with
the harp-strings, and perchance, the melodies have not quite
left memory barren [Gwen. *startled*). Bring me a harp, and
I will try and do something for Lady Gwenllian's diversion.
(*Applause*).
EDN. (*Coming to front ; harp is brought, sings* " Farewell of
Ednyfed." *After* 1st *stanza* Gwen *approaches, looks at him
intently*).
GWEN. Art thou Ednyfed ? Art thou my long-lost Prince ?
EDN. What maketh thee think that this poor minstrel is the
lord and master of this fine palace ? Let me on with my
song. (*Sings another stanza : excitement !*)
GWEN. (*rushing forward*). None other than Ednyfed could
sing that song. Thou art 'Nyfed ? Tell me, tell me, for
mercy's sake !
EDN. (*All crowding*). Yes, my Gwen. (*She throws herself into
his arms*). I am thy lost, thy long lost husband. The
reason of my long absence I will tell thee presently. But
(*pointing to* Iorwerth), who is this hawk who seeks to make

d

his nest within mine ? Which wouldst thou, Gwenno ?
Leave me and this my once happy home or stay ? Take thy
choice ! I will give thee time to think whilst I rehearse to
this man's assembled guests and thine the reason of my
absence. (*Bridegroom elect makes for the door.*) Stop him !
(Madoc *and others bar the way*). It needs be that things be
explained.

GWEN (*throwing herself into his arms*). 'Nyfed, 'Nyfed, I am
thine always, and have been, and will be now and for ever.
I believed thee dead.

EDN. I am alive enough to feather yon cockerel, if needs be,
but he is not worthy of the honour ! However, I want him
and all assembled to hear the real cause of my absence . . . .
Now, my Lady Gwenllian, and my friends all, let me explain
my strange absence. Many fights I fought unscathed, but
at the last I was struck down by a treacherous blow. In-
sensible was I carried off the battlefield, and, when my mind
cleared, I found myself within a dungeon I knew not where.
For years was I incarcerated there and badly treated, just
kept alive and no more. One day there entered my prison-
house the Lord of the castle, and would have conference
with me—a stately man and of sound sense. (*Turning to*
Gwen.) Gwen, remembrest thou that *ring* taken off the
drowned sailor's hand ?

GWEN. Yes, 'Nyfed, well do I remember it. Thou gavest it to
me and I to thee at thy departure. But what of it ?

EDN. It may sound strange, it saved my life.

MEGAN. I was sure there was something strange about that
glittering jewel.

EDN. Well, to continue my tale :—Thou remembrest also our
compact about the stars (Gwen *nods*). In my dungeon I
could never see the stars, and therefore I wore the ring at
night, which, with the slightest light, shone like a star. I
had it on when the Lord of the Castle came in. He asked me
sundry questions—whence I was ?—my position ?—my
estates, and many things pertinent to my coming to Palestine.
When suddenly he leaped at me, caught me by the hand, and
cried :—Thou villain, how camest thou by this my ring ?
These ten years have I lost it. Thou shalt surely die. (*All
listen*). I explained the circumstances——the wrecks, the

inundation, and, thou knowest, the finding of the ring on the foreigner's hand. He believed me, and was so overjoyed, that forthwith upon restoration of the ring, which doubtless had been stolen from him, he said :—That ring hath talismanic power ! Hence it saves thy life. The spirit of Allah dwells within it, and shines through it. It hath kept thee all these years. I take back my talisman ; take thou back thy liberty, and with his own hand unlocked he the prison door ! Nay more, he placed his purse in my hand, which contained some monies sufficient to keep me at any rate from starvation in my great struggle to gain Llys Euryn once more. My great regret is that Gwilym, my faithful loyal shield bearer, is no more. He was killed at the same time that I was stricken. I can only hope he had burial.

GWEN (*much affected*). Poor Gwilym ! Sad it is to think that never more shall his serious, but kindly face be seen at Llys Euryn.

EDN. It is so, alas ! and methinks I returned none too soon.

GWEN. My Prince, we thought thee dead ; we did in truth.

EDN. I would not blame thee, my dear one. I feel that thou art real and true. (*Turning to* Iorwerth). Serpent, thou hast heard her choice. Now begone, and let me not set eyes on thee again, for fear that something untoward befall thee by the way.

IOR. I fear thee not, and will meet thee whenever thou wilt.

EDN. Thou rat ! thou art in my house. I release the foul thing. Begone ! Madoc see him hence. (*Turning to* Gwen). Gwen, my own, we are once more re-united. Heaven be praised for bringing me back in the hour of need.

GWEN. (*nestling up to him*). Yes, in truth may heaven be praised !

MEGAN (*coming forward*). Said I not that he, my Prince, would come back ? And said I not that the ring would work for weal or woe to Llys Euryn ?

EDN. Thou art as superstitious as ever, thou dear old bundle of all that's good and faithful (*patting her on the back*). I would not part with thee for many flocks of sheep.

MADOC (*looking foolish*). Craving your mercy my returned and beloved Master, seeing that my Lady Gwenllian was about to take to herself another husband, Megan and Madoc have arranged to—er—to —er— that we would end——

EDN. (*roaring with laughter*). What ? Megan, you a spritely bride and you Madoc a prancing bridegroom ! Oh lads and lasses ! !

MADOC (*good humouredly*). I will keep to my bargain.

MEGAN. And I to mine, though he is a clumsy cormorant, who knows naught except how to catch fish.

EDN. (*jocularly*). He has caught thee at any rate. Madoc, my man, thou hast a weighty one here ! Be circumspect, Madoc ! do not draw in the rope too quickly or too tightly, or the tackle will break. Ah well, *young* people must have their way in these things ! However, you must both of you live on as before beneath Llys Euryn rafters, or I will not give my consent (*smiling*).

MEGAN. My Prince, my heart would break if I had to leave your service.

EDN. Tut ! Tut ! Thou hast no heart now. Thou hast lost it. (Madoc *giggles*). Come, Gwenno, and all of you, let us to the gardens once more. How glorious to be in my native land and in my home once more. Come, Gwen (*arm round waist*).   [*All exeunt finally.*

THE END.

THE REV. T. E. TIMOTHY.

OLWEN

OF THE

MONKS' WEIR.

A TALE OF RHOS FYNACH AND OF THE FISHING WEIR AT
RHOS-ON-SEA.

DRAMATIS PERSONÆ.

FATHER CYNAN		Prior of Rhôs Fynach.
HYWEL		
IORWERTH		
DEWI		Monks of Rhôs Fynach.
RODERIG		
CARADOG		
ROGER		A Black Friar.
MAELGWYN, LORD PENDARAN ..		A Welsh Nobleman.
LORD GREY		A nobleman of Dorset.
DUKE OF SOMERSET		Minister of King Henry VIII.
MADOC		Son of Lord Pendaran.
TWM OF RHYD		Welsh farmer.
GWILYM DINARTH		Body-servant of Lord Pendaran.
MYFANWY		Fisher-girl.
MALI		Wife of Twm of Rhyd.
LADY BRENDA		Wife of Lord Pendaran.
OLWEN		Daughter of Lord Grey.

Monks, peasants, fisherfolk, attendants, soldiers, and village
children.

ACT I.

SCENE.—Grounds attached to Rhos Fynach.
Time : In the year 1536.

*Enter a number of monks, who have just returned from fishing
the Weir, and some of whom still carry the nets.*

FATHER IORWERTH (*joyfully*).

What a splendid catch was that we had this tide, and
what exciting sport it was to land some of the salmon !
Methinks the sea must be full of evil spirits, the way the

salmon leap sometimes,—like men possessed they twist and wriggle and leap in all directions !

Father Hywel. Possessed with demons or terrorised by monks, life in this monastery would be dull and monotonous enough but for this excitement of fishing which this weir provideth for us ! By the rood, in my heart I often sing a ' Jubilate,' when, tired with my devotions or my work in the garden, the summons is given, that it is my turn to do the fishing.

Father Iorwerth. Marry, of a truth, just cause have *we*, the monks of Rhos Fynach, to bless the memory of good Abbot Ieuan of Conwy, whose fertile brain devised this cunning method of catching fish ! By my faith, had I for a moment the power and authority of the Blessed Pope, I would canon-ise this good Abbot, and appoint a day in the Calendar, wherein to sing his virtues and to recall the origin of this fishing weir. By the memory of St. Garmon ! men have been canonised for less service to mankind, than that which this most reverend Abbot rendered to the people of his day.

Father Dewi (*eagerly*). Pray tell me, brother Iorwerth, how the Abbot Ieuan came to construct this Weir !

Father Iorwerth (*with surprise*). Methought everyone knew the history of the Weir ! Thou must know that in the time of the first Richard, King of England, a host of Saxon robbers ravaged our land, destroying everything before them until Llewellyn ap Iorwerth arose, ' that eagle of men that loveth not to lie nor to sleep,' as one of our bards describeth him, and drove them like chaff before the blast of a hurricane back to their own land. Like sheep, it is said, these Saxon robbers fled before the fierce wolf that crested his red helmet of battle. Following these ravages of the Saxons there came a great famine, and the cry of anguish was heard throughout the land. Men, women and children gathered daily around the monasteries, and the monks were greatly perplexed as to what to do to help the poor people. The learned Abbot Ieuan of Conwy, whose knowledge of the tides was great, while spending a night at Rhos Fynach, bethought him of placing a weir in the course of the tide that sweepeth from Penmaen to Môn, for the efforts of the fisher-folk of Glanymor to meet the demands of the hungry people for fish, had lately been attended with but little success. The story goeth on to relate that at sight of the shoal of fish that followed the first drawing of the weir, the people, joyous beyond control over their deliverance from starvation, rushed to Rhos Fynach and almost worshipped good Abbot Ieuan, whom they found kneeling in the oratory, praying for the success of his device.

ALL THE MONKS.   Blessed be his memory !

FATHER HYWEL (*enthusiastically*).   Ay, blessed be his memory ! not only for the relief he secured for the famine-stricken people of his day, but also for the excitement and merriment which his contrivance hath given to the generations of monks that have dwelt at Rhos Fynach since his time. Dost remember, brother Iorwerth, the laughter we enjoyed only yesterday, over the excitement of Twm of Rhyd, who ever forsaketh his work to watch the fishing, and how he sought to hold that big salmon ?

FATHER IORWERTH (*laughingly*).   Marry, do I.   Ha ! ha ! and after the salmon had slipped through his hands well-nigh a dozen times, how he at last sat on the poor fish, muttering to himself as he did so, that he was not going to be beaten by any salmon.   Ha !   Ha !   (*The other monks join in his laughter*).

FATHER HYWEL.   Ay, and I warrant me, that he received the length of his wife's tongue when he reached home.   Sancta Maria ! they tell me that her tongue, like the sea around us, is never still, and that its flow is almost always like that of the *wintry* sea, threatening and sweeping aside all that try to withstand it.

FATHER IORWERTH (*smilingly*).   There never was thy like for gossip, brother Hywel, and how thine ear getteth to hear it puzzleth me.   Methinks thou must question all the village folk thou meetest, even as I have heard thee question our beloved Olwen.   *She* it is true, can tell thee much, for she knoweth every soul in the district, and there is not a home that doth not give her a welcome.   By my faith, though, I warrant *she* speaketh *evil* of no one, but only *good*, for her mind hath been too well trained to harbour evil thoughts. Somehow, when she visiteth Rhos Fynach, it is thy jovial face she seeketh, after paying her respects to our reverend

Prior, and to thee she discloseth the pleasures and worries of the world around us. The faces of the rest of us, I trow, are too sober and too solemn to attract a winsome maid, though there is not one brother here that would not go through fire and water to serve Olwen.

FATHER HYWEL (*pleased, but waiving aside the compliment*). No, No, brother Iorwerth, abuse not thine own kind face and the faces of my brother monks. Know that Olwen, the maid of the Weir, hath a peculiar affection for me, because I was the one who first discovered her ; and, by our Lady, she oweth me much for the great terror with which she filled me, when the sea gave her up to us ! And, in truth, she seeketh me out too, because she knoweth I love a *little* gossip, and what maid or woman is there, that liketh not to impart gossip to willing ears ?

FATHER RODERIG (*eagerly*). Ah, brother Hywel, now that thou hast mentioned the finding of Olwen, wilt thou, of thy goodness, give me the full story ? It happened before I joined the Order, and my brothers here, I dare say, will not be wearied of the story, even though they may have heard thee repeat it before.

FATHER DEWI. It is a tale that I, for one, never tire of hearing.

FATHER HYWEL. I may tell thee, brother Roderig, that it is a story I love not overmuch to repeat owing to the terror it recalleth to my mind, but to please thee, I will give thee the tale. Brother Iorwerth can tell thee how the experience affrighted me—

FATHER IORWERTH (*interrupting*). Ay, and by my sooth, I can tell him that thou wast not the only one that was terrified that night !

FATHER HYWEL (*with much agitation and many gestures as he proceeds with his tale*). The terror of that night overtaketh me *now* at times—and when the scene is repeated in my sleep, as is the case sometimes, I wake up to find my hard cot damp with the perspiration of fear that hath flowed from me. Know then, brother Roderig, that it was my turn one night many years ago, to fish the weir. Brother Iorwerth and two or three other brother monks had also been deputed to the task, but in my haste I started long before the others, and alone arrived at the Weir. It must be told thee, that the

night before there had been a furious gale from the West, and
I was wondering how much damage, if any, had been done to
the weir ; finding the water too deep to use my nets, I
looked about, by the aid of a lantern, to discover whether
the sides of the weir had suffered through the violence of the
gale. (*He pauses, looking somewhat agitated*). I had just
moved forward, when, Sancta Maria ! from the end of the
weir there issued the cry of a little child, the wail as of an
infant crying for comfort . . . . Terror fixed me to the sand
I stood on . . . . I could not move . . . . I felt my tonsure
rising, as if some invisible hand were lifting it from my
skull . . . . . The dampness of fear spread over my whole
body . . . . Again, the wailing cry of a child was heard
above the noise of the wash of the sea, and at the sound my
knees gave way under me, my lantern dropped, and I was
crossing myself violently and calling on all the saints in the
Calendar to help me . . . . . Again was the cry heard, and
by a superhuman effort I rose and fled, fled for Rhos Fynach,
heeding neither the falls nor the sharp stones that hindered
my progress. (*He pauses to recover himself*).
When I reached my brother monks, who were just starting
with their nets, I told them what I had heard, They laughed scornfully, and said I was not yet awake and had been
dreaming, and that it was the sound of the wind whistling
through the wattled cage of the weir that I had heard.   I
allowed myself to be persuaded that this was the explanation
of the cry I had heard, and so, insisting on our taking all the
lanterns we could find, I returned with them to the weir.
By that time, the water had receded much, and one could go
much farther in to the weir, and not a sound except that of
the wash of the waves had been heard.   My companions
were beginning to laugh at the recollection of my terror,
when, again, the same wailing cry was heard, and we all
stood, stilled and silenced with the numbness of fear . . .
Not a whisper could one of us utter, while still the wailing
cries went on . . . . At last one recovered himself, and then
another, and another ; and, fortified by the courage which
numbers impart, we went boldly into the weir to discover
the cause—and there, caught by one of the stakes of the
weir, hung a leathern basket, and within could be

observed the form of a child, well-protected from the cold, and tied to its cradle. Not a murmur did we make, but leaving there our nets, and forgetful of our fishing, we hastened with our strange burden to our reverend Prior—

FATHER RODERIG (*interrupting*). And did none of you first undo the wraps that covered the child—

FATHER HYWEL (*breaking in*). No, we deemed it best for our reverend Prior to be the one to examine into the matter; *he*, amazed at our disturbing his sleep, and still more amazed at our story, came hastily, and undoing the wraps, disclosed to our gaze, a child, as beauteous to behold as the fairest flower of the field. (*Pause, and then with relief*). *There* you have the story of the finding of Olwen.

FATHER RODERIG. I thank thee, brother Hywel, for thy interesting story. But, an it pleases thee, tell me what further you did.

FATHER HYWEL. Our most reverend father, discerning from the clothes and from the crest that adorned them, that she was a child of noble birth, and had probably been committed to the mercy of Him that controleth the sea, by parents or guardians undergoing shipwreck during the storm I spoke of, went during the morning to good Lady Brenda of Llys Euryn, and asked her to rear the child, informing her that a child thus miraculously preserved, would prove a blessing to all who were kind to her.

FATHER IORWERTH (*warmly*). And true words of prophecy he spoke, for a blessing hath she been to all who have known her. Like a bright sunbeam she peepeth into every home cheering all around. At Rhos Fynach, as everyone knoweth, she is at all times greatly welcomed. She looketh up to our most reverend Prior as unto a saint, while amongst us the sound of her laughter and the cheering note of her voice are as music after gloom and woe.

FATHER DEWI. Ay, and unto the Lady Brenda she is as a beloved daughter, and a source of comfort and joy to all at Llys Euryn.

FATHER HYWEL. Methinks she will present herself here to-day. It is one of the days when she cometh craving fish for some of her sick folk. I hope she will come, as I desire to know what form the village festivities are going to take to-morrow, for she, I warrant, hath taken the matter in hand, and, with the village folk, what she commandeth is done.

FATHER RODERIG. Festivities! what festivities dost thou refer to, brother Hywel?

FATHER HYWEL. Hast thou forgotten that to-morrow is the festival of St. Trillo, the patron of the Church on the hill? Evident is it that thou dost not allow thy mind to dwell on festivities, or thou wouldst not have forgotten the day of St. Trillo, for to the folk of Glanymor is it a time of much merriment. Methinks we all should go and join in the festivities. But (*seeing* brother Caradog *approaching the grounds*) what aileth brother Caradog that he hasteth here with so eager a step? His countenance bodeth ill news!

FATHER CARADOG. I haste to tell ye all that Friar Roger hath arrived and is now having an audience with our reverend Prior. As I passed the oratory I saw them both, engaged in earnest talk, and from their anxious faces, I fear Friar Roger hath brought ill news. But here they come. (*The* Prior and Friar Roger *are seen approaching talking earnestly to each other. They greet the monks with* a 'Benedicite' *and* 'Pax vobiscum').

PRIOR CYNAN. I grieve, my brethren, to tell you that Friar Roger, who hath travelled here from Caerleon is the bearer of ill news—news that disturbeth and will disturb every monastery in the land, for, by order of the King's Minister, Thomas Cromwell, all the lesser monasteries are to be suppressed, and my fears are great that Rhos Fynach will be destroyed, and our quiet community scattered.

ALL THE MONKS (*disturbed and downcast*). Saint Mary preserve us!

FRIAR ROGER (*fiercely and with much agitation*). Ay, the fear of Cromwell hath mastered both King and people. Tyranny and bloodshed are over-spreading the land. His cursed spies are scattered far and wide. People go about in fear, and tread silently and carefully, 'as if a scorpion lay sleeping under every stone, ready at the least noise to spring and sting them.'

FATHER HYWEL. The holy Saints aid us!

FATHER RODERIG (*in great surprise*). Dareth this Cromwell, the disciple of his excellency Cardinal Wolsey, to persecute the Church?

FRIAR ROGER (*fiercely*). Dareth ?   Verily, there is nothing or
no one that this minister dare not attack.   Men go about in
fear and dread . . . . . ' Words idly spoken are tortured
into treason.' . . . . The blood that staineth the block of
execution is never dry . . . . Far and wide his arm reacheth
and his minions seize the noblest in the land.   The most
learned of your fraternity are being accused of treason, so
that he may have cause for laying hand on their goods.   At
this present time the *lesser* monasteries are being suppressed,
and their lands given over to the king—soon the *greater*
monasteries will follow, for the spirit of robbery and rapine
once awakened resteth not, until the last groat hath been
taken.   Perdition seize this minister, that seeketh to spoil—
PRIOR CYNAN (*interrupting*).   Hush, Friar Roger, prophesy
not so darkly of the destinies of our Church, and speak not
so bitterly of this minister, however great his enmity to our
sacred order may be, for the creed of Holy Church forbiddeth
her sons to speak so.
FRIAR ROGER.   Speak !   most reverend Prior, my blood boileth
within me, at the remembrance of what I saw as I travelled
from Caerefrog to Caerleon !   Hadst *thou* seen, as I have
seen, the poor that used to be fed at the monasteries now
seeking food in vain, thou, gentle as thou art, wouldst speak
as I speak !   Is there the spirit of justice in the law that
robbeth the Church of the land and monies that her pious
sons and daughters in the past have left to her use, in order
that the coffers of a greedy minister may be filled, and the
coffers of the king that minister serveth ?   No ! such a law
insulteth high Heaven !   May his pride and ambition soon
bring this tyrant minister to his fall !   May he soon be
brought to the block whither he hath sent so many of the
noblest and most learned of our land !   And as for the dis-
solute king he serveth—may his children be childless, so
that the line of the Tudors come soon to an end—may
PRIOR CYNAN (*interrupting*).   Friar Roger, I must command
thee to be silent.   Verily, thy zeal for Holy Church hath
bereft thee of thy reason, and hath caused thy words to
savour of wickedness.   Serve the Church in the way thou
hast chosen, and pursue thy preaching and thy seeking for
the lost.   As long as the law of the land alloweth *us*, we shall

abide where we are, carrying gentle peace in our hands to silence those that wish evil to the Church, praying for the people, helping them when they call, and trusting to the noblemen and people around to help us protect our land. I thank thee for warning us of our danger. But now, go thy way. Refresh thyself at the refectory, and continue thy task of warning other monasteries. Thy hot zeal and fierce wrath disturb our peace, and the even flow of our ways.

FRIAR ROGER. Fare thee well, most reverend Prior, and ye, my brethren. Pray that the people and the noblemen ye trust fail you not in the hour of trial that is threatening you. Fare ye well. (*Exit.*)

PRIOR CYNAN (*turning to the monks*). Methinks that in Friar Roger will be shown the truth of that proverb, ' Never Friar forgot feud.' It is, forsooth, disturbing news that he hath brought us, and it behoveth us to pray for help and guidance. But, ah! (*seeing* Olwen *approaching*) here cometh Olwen, our beloved child.

Enter Olwen *running toward the* Prior *and kneeling before him to receive a silent blessing.*

PRIOR CYNAN. Arise, my child, we bid thee welcome. As sunshine after fierce storm is thy coming now, so soon after the departing of the good but fiery Friar Roger.

OLWEN (*first turning to the assembled monks and saying* ' Good morrow to ye all,' *and then addressing the* Prior. I thank thee, most reverend Father. Thou art always ready with a courteous word. What news hath Friar Roger brought, for you all appear sad and downcast.

PRIOR CYNAN. Sad and troublous, my daughter, hath the news been, which the good Friar brought, but thou art too young to have thy mind disturbed by the news of the outer world. Well, what good errand hath brought thee here ?

OLWEN. I came to see whether any fish have been caught at the weir to-day, for I would have thee give me some to take to old Sara Ty Gwyn, who is old and bed-ridden. And (*turning to* Father Hywel,) I wanted to remind thee, Father Hywel, of the Festival of S. Trillo, and to tell thee that there will be singing and dancing and games at the festivities to-morrow, and I hope thou and thy brothers will be present, for I am to be the Queen of the day.

PRIOR CYNAN. We thank thee, good daughter, for thinking of us. Thou art always ready to introduce brightness into our quiet life. But know, that if we come not to the village green to-morrow, the news Friar Roger brought, hath much disquieted us, and that we shall be at our shrine offering prayers for a way of escape from the trouble that now threateneth us. Fare thee well, my daughter. Give our affections to the good people of Llys Euryn, and ask at the buttery for the fish thou requirest for thy sick. Fare thee well.

OLWEN. Fare ye well, all. I trust ye will all come to the morrow's festival, for it will grieve the village folk not to see you on the village green. (*Exit.*)

PRIOR CYNAN. And now, my brethren, before we seek our several cells to engage in prayer to our Lady for the salvation of our Church from persecution, we will all sing the prayer of good St. Trillo.*

They all sing :—

> Bugail y praidd, Corlanydd hoff yr wyn,
> Tydi ein Llyw yn ngwyll dymestlog nôs,
> Meddyg ein clwyf, O gwrando ar ein cwyn,
> Tywys ein camrau ac i'n cymmorth dôs,
> > Meddyg ein clwyf, O gwrando ar ein cwyn,
> > Tywys ein camrau, O dwg, dwg ni adref.
>
> Crwydrasom oll, pa le mae'r gorlan glyd,
> Gysgodol nyth i'r sawl a'i ceisiant hi ?
> Lle saif y Groes, yn euraidd grair o hyd—
> Adgoffydd ing, ffynnonell bythol fri,
> > Lle saif y Groes yn euraidd grair o hyd,
> > Ffynnonell bythol fri—dwg ni adref.

(*Exeunt.*)

END OF ACT I.

---

* Words of ' Shepherd of Souls ' by Wilson Barratt, translated by Rev. E, James Evans.

ACT II.

SCENE.—Village Green.   Maypole in centre ready for the dance.

Time.   Early in the afternoon of St. Trillo's Day.

Enter Mali *of Rhyd Farm, talking excitedly to* Myfanwy *the fisher-girl.*

MALI.   Hast seen my good man anywhere about Glanymor ? He left the farm at noon in the midst of his work, and to enjoy himself, I warrant.   An he but hear of any festivities, he leaveth the farm to see to itself, and then blameth me if anything goeth wrong.   Why did I ever marry ?

MYFANWY.   Mali anwyl, excite not thyself.   Thy good-man Twm loveth to help with any festivities, and even now thou mayest find him at Aberhod preparing the children for their appearance on the green, and thou knowest full well that wert thou a young maid tomorrow, and Twm came to thee with his pleasing tongue, thou wouldst be as ready to wed him as thou wert years ago.

MALI.   Ay, Twm was ever sweet of tongue, but were his tongue made of honey, it would take him long to get me to consent to wed him, after what I have learnt of married life !   By my sooth, once a maid marrieth, care and worry become her portion all the day long.   'Fanwy take my advice, never get wed.

FANWY.   In truth, thy work cannot have gone well this day at Rhyd, that thou speakest so.   But (*shyly*) it is somewhat late to proffer me this advice of thine.

MALI.   Mercy o' me !   I had forgotten that thou wert betrothed to Gwilym of Dinarth that serveth the Lord Pendaran, and wert soon to wed with him.   Eh, young maids are foolish !   Anything wearing the garb of a man strutting past, and they straightway *fly* to his embraces !

MYFANWY.   Thou seem'st to forget that thou wast once a maid !

MALI.   Ay, but it is now that I know how foolish I was.   *There* was I in peace and comfort at Llys Euryn, happy in nursing Mistress Olwen and Master Madoc who were then but babes, and *there* I might have ended my days, only that Twm came a courting me and singing my praises, and would not rest until I had consented to wed him.

MYFANWY. O Mali, thou knowest thou wert as bad as Twm—

MALI. Bad as Twm, indeed ! Why, he never left me in peace, but followed me wherever I went. He said I would never have to work as mistress of Rhyd Farm. He was going to see to everything. Now, I know better. Ah, how different men are before and after marriage ! Before thou art wed thy man will do anything for thee. He will buy thee jewels of gold, and jewels of silver—he will buy thee coloured ribbons, and take thee to all the festivals, but once thou art wed, he grumbleth at buying thee anything or at taking thee anywhere—No, no, thou hast to stay at home, and see that everything goeth on as it should, and—

MYFANWY (*interrupting*) Oh, Mali, I shall not listen to thee— Gwilym will not be like *thy* good-man, Gwilym is different to Twm !

MALI (*indignantly*). Different to Twm, forsooth ! Know, thou saucy maid, that there is not a kinder or a better husband than Twm in all the country round ; and as for looks, there was not a more handsome than Twm in all the district of Dinarth in the days when he courted me on the slopes of Bryn Euryn !

MYFANWY (*laughing*). O Mali, Mali, well knew I that I had but to speak badly of Twm, and thou wouldst be angry at once, and speak well of thy goodman. Twm is beloved of everyone for his goodwill and kindness, and as for the good monks of Rhos Fynach, they will do anything for Twm of Rhyd !

MALI (*mollified somewhat*). Ay, methinks, Twm is over fond of these same monks. He would think more of his farm, but for these monks, for they call him to come to the fishing at the weir, just to see his excitement, and to laugh at him. Thou shouldst have seen the state Twm was in, only the day before yesterday, after being at that weir. He came home wet through, his clothes torn, and carrying a salmon that looked as if it had been between the grindstones of the mill, but which, it seemeth, Twm had in his great excitement sat on.

MYFANWY (*laughingly*). Ha ! ha ! How the good monks must have enjoyed seeing him ! But— Oh, there cometh Mistress Olwen, and with her Master Madoc.

Enter Olwen *and* Madoc *both running to greet their old nurse*
Mali.

OLWEN (*joyfully and excitedly*). O Mali, I am pleased that thou
hast been able to come to the festival, for I am to be the
Queen of the day. After the dancing on the green, all the
village folk and children are to go to Llys Euryn to partake
of the festal meal given by the Lord Pendaran and the Lady
Brenda, and to-night there is to be a bonfire on the top of
Bryn Euryn !

MALI. Thy active brain I warrant hath been at work devising
these festivities ! and how is my young master ?

MADOC. I am well, I thank thee. (*Joyfully*). And Mali ! I
am to attend on the Queen this day, and this night I am to
light the bon-fire !

OLWEN. O Mali ! and where is Twm ? Hast thou left him at
the farm ? And how are the six calves, and the twelve
little pigs, and the hundred young ducks and chickens, and—

MALI. Hold, hold, my young mistress, thou wilt make one
think that Rhyd is an ark of refuge whither all animals come
to give birth to their young !   Twm is at Aberhod, and, I
warrant, worketh hard in preparing the children for thy
procession !

MYFANWY. Are the Lord Pendaran and the Lady Brenda
going to honour the Festival with their presence, for the
children love to see them and the monks of Rhos
Fynach, at their festivities ?

OLWEN. Lord Pendaran and the Lady Brenda are even now
on their way, but I fear me the monks of Rhos Fynach will
not come. Bad news hath reached them, the nature of
which I know not, but which will keep them from coming
hither to the village green. But, come, Madoc, we must
haste to Aberhod, for the children await us.

(*Exeunt* Olwen *and* Madoc, *running*).

MYFANWY. I tell thee what, Mali, some day those two will wed,
thou wilt see !

MALI. Thy mind ever runneth on love ! But, by my sooth, I
hope thy words will come true, for Mistress Olwen and
Master Madoc be well-suited, and should they wed, no
palace in the land will have a better lord to rule it. or a
more beautiful lady to grace it !

MYFANWY (*thoughtfully*). I suppose it will never be known
whose child Mistress Olwen is.

MALI. Some great lord's, *I warrant*. No one that knoweth
that child as I do, can doubt that. Ah ! (*seeing* Twm *and*
Gwilym Dinarth *approaching*) there's that truant Twm and
with him Gwilym Dinarth !

(*Enter* Twm *and* Gwilym *to prepare the green for the children's
dance, etc.* Gwilym *seeing* Myfanwy *greeteth her with the
words*, Ah, Myfanwy, anwylyd, *and they retire to a corner of
the stage, holding each other's hands and whispering*).

TWM ((*loudly*). Hallo, Mali, cariad, I never expected to find
thee here so soon !

MALI. No, I warrant, thou lazy-bones ! Thou wouldst keep
me at Rhyd, wouldst thou not, working whilst thou art enjoying thyself ?

TWM. Hush, Mali, give us the *sweet* side of thy tongue on this
festal day, the side thou didst always give me when I courted
thee on the slopes of Bryn Eruyn. Nowadays, thou seemest
to delight in giving me the *rough* side of thy tongue.

MALI. (*angrily*). An thou hadst to feed a dozen pigs, six calves,
a hundred chicks——

TWM (*interrupting angrily*). Tut ! tut ! prepared I not all the
food before I went out ? Thou hadst but to place the food
before the animals—but, there, what availeth it to talk to an
angry wife ! How different women are before and after
marriage !

MALI (*scornfully*). Different, say'st thou, not more different
than men !

TWM (*angrily*). Aye, different. Before marriage they are like
the Rose-bush that bloometh even now at Rhos Fynach—
beauteous to look at, soft to the touch, and sweetening the
air around—but after marriage, they are like that bush in
the autumn, the colours faded, the sweetness gone, and
touch it—thou art pricked by the thorns that before were
hidden from the eye !

MALI. Oh, that I should live to hear myself likened to a bush
of thorns—I, the once honoured servant at Llys Euryn and
the loved nurse of its children ! (*She weeps*).

TWM (*placing his arm round her and speaking soothingly*). There,
Mali anwyl, I did not mean to speak to thee like that. Thou

knowest I love thee, as much as ever I did in the old days on
Bryn Euryn. Thou art the best wife in the whole of Dinarth—thy good qualities are my boast at every
gathering of men. Forgive me, Mali, I spoke roughly because
my mind is troubled over some bad news I have heard—

MALI (*looking lovingly at him*). Twm anwyl, it was my fault.
After thou didst leave Rhyd to-day, everything went wrong,
and my temper hath been bad ever since. But what bad
news hast thou heard ?

TWM. It was news about Rhos Fynach. As I went to
Aberhod, I met Father Hywel, and he told me that Rhos
Fynach was in danger of being taken from them through the
order of the King, and that the monks would not thus be at
the Festivities this day—but, away with news that dis-
pleaseth—needs must Gwilym and I place the throne in
readiness for the Queen—Gwilym, leave thy Myfanwy, and
help me place the throne for the Queen—

(Twm *and* Gwilym *place everything ready for the children, while*
Mali *and* Myfanwy *look on, whispering and smiling*).

*A sound of a bugle is heard, and enter soon after two boys
dressed as heralds, one of whom shouts,* ' Make way, make
way, for the Queen of the Day.'

*Enter the Procession, as follows :—eight little girls dressed as
daffodil fairies, six or eight peasant girls, six boys dressed as
fisher-lads, drawing a small flower-bedecked carriage wherein
sits* Olwen *as the* Queen ; *at each side of the carriage walk two
or more boys dressed as archers ; immediately behind the
carriage* Madoc *as* Prince ; *behind* Madoc *six or more girls
dressed as Court ladies, and behind all, fisher-folk, and peasants
ad lib. followed by* Lord Pendaran *and* Lady Brenda *with
attendants from* Llys Euryn.

The Queen *being seated on the throne, and with all the young
revellers arranged picturesquely around her, says,* ' Let the
revels now proceed.

*As many dancers as are required step forward and dance a
Morris dance or arrange themselves round the May-pole, and
give the May-pole dance.*

*At its conclusion all huzza and cheer, while intermingled
with the cheers, are shouts,* ' The Queen ! the Queen ! ' *and,*
' The Song of St. Trillo ! the song of S. Trillo ! '

In response to the cries, the Queen *stands in her carriage, bows to all, and sings the* 'Song of St. Trillo,'* *all her attendant revellers joining in the chorus.*

I.

Our good St. Trillo we invoke
  On this his Festal Day ;
To him, the friend of all poor folk,
  We'll sing a merry lay.
He blesses all—the young and old,
  The matron and the maid,
The sailor brave, the warrior bold,
  Who have their votives paid.

Chorus.

Then once and twice and three times hail ! ! !
  Come, shout it with a will—
To the bless'd Saint who does not fail
  The Church upon the hill.

2

With empty net and saddened brow
  The fisher seeks the shore,
There to St. Trillo pays his vow,
  Then launches forth once more ;
For when the Saint's benignant smile
  Irradiates the deep,
The fishes, yielding to his guile,
  Into the draw-net leap.

Chorus.

Then once and twice and three times hail ! ! !
  Come, shout it with a will—
To the bless'd Saint who will not fail
  The fisher's net to fill.

3

With sweet, sad mien the loving maid,
  In Cupid's fetters bound,
With deep-drawn sigh implores his aid
  That true her swain be found ;

---

* Written by Rev. E. James Evans, to the air 'Dydd Gwyl Dewi (St. David's Day).

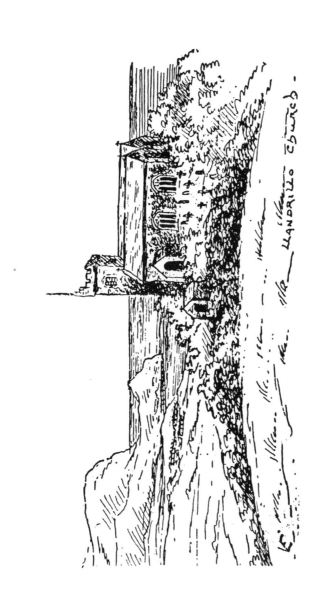

Llandrillo Church.

For well she knows that our good Saint
   Will pity her distress,
And turn to weal her earnest plaint
   Should he but deign to bless—

Chorus.
   Then once and twice and three times hail ! ! !
     Come, shout it with a will—
   To our bless'd Saint who cannot fail
     Her cup of love to fill.

4

The husbandmen, who sow in rain
   May hope to reap in shine ;
The good old Saint will bring them gain
   Who worship at his shrine ;
Their cattle will increase the more,
   Like patriarchal stock,
Who on St. Trillo's Day implore
   The Saint to bless the flock.

Chorus.
   Then once and twice and three times hail ! ! !
     Come, shout it with a will—
   To the bless'd Saint who does not fail
     The Church upon the hill.

At the conclusion of the song, all the revellers cheer, and with the cheers there are heard the cries, ' A dance, a dance,' and if the Queen and the attendant Prince are able, they should dance a pavan or a measure or some dance of the period of Henry VIII. ; or, all the children may take part in some dance resembling Lancers, or Sir Roger de Coverley, or some simple dance of the period of Henry VIII.

At the conclusion of the dance the Lord Pendaran *steps forward, and bowing to the* Queen, *says—*

I thank thy gracious Majesty for thy song, and you her faithful subjects for the joyous revels which the Lady Brenda and I have much enjoyed. And now, the Lady Brenda and I would feel honoured if Her Majesty the Queen of S. Trillo's Day, and her subjects would partake of the refreshments provided for them at Llys Euryn.

MADOC (*majestically*). My Lord Pendaran, and my Lady Brenda, on behalf of the Queen, I beg to thank you for your gracious invitation, and to say that Her Majesty the Queen and her subjects will be pleased to proceed at once to Llys Euryn.

(Cheers from the revellers).

The Buglers sounding the call, a procession is formed as before, and all exeunt.

END OF ACT II.

ACT III.

SCENE.—Grounds at Llys Euryn.
Time—Early in the evening of St. Trillo's Day.

Enter the Lord Pendaran *and the* Lady Brenda.

LORD PENDARAN (*seriously*). The time hath come, Brenda, when it must be settled one way or the other, as to what must be done with Olwen—

LADY BRENDA (*grieved*). Oh, Maelgwyn, art going to worry thyself over that theme again ? Surely there is sufficient time—

LORD PENDARAN (*interrupting impatiently*). Sufficient time, No ! No ! Evident was it to anyone seeing those two this afternoon on the festal green, that, growing up together as they do, they are bound to fall in love and, however well they may be suited to each other, still it behoveth me not to permit my son Modoc, in whose veins courseth the blood of the Cymric Kings, to wed with one of whose parentage nothing is known. (*In decisive tones*) We must separate the two ere it be too late !

LADY BRENDA (*very much hurt*). O Maelgwyn, how thou hurtest me when thou speakest that way ! I love Olwen as much as I love my son Modoc. My heart telleth me (and the heart of a mother never erreth where her own son is concerned), that Olwen cometh of a family that would not disgrace that of Maelgwyn Pendaran, proud though it be !

LORD PENDARAN. Brenda, my beloved, I grieve to disturb thee. I, too, have learnt to love this foster-daughter of mine—but this separation must be effected. Modoc shall be sent to my kinsman Owain of Powys, to learn the art of war ; thence he shall be sent to the Court. Perchance,

seeing the world will make my son forget Olwen, and the
vows which, I trow, he, young though he be, hath already
formed in his heart, to wed her, when he cometh to man's
estate.

LADY BRENDA (*pleadingly*). Maelgwyn beloved, why art thou
so proud ?   Seeing that we both love Olwen, would it not be
well to make her our daughter in very truth ?

LORD PENDARAN. Venture on this course I cannot !   Should
it, in after years, transpire that Olwen was not of gentle
blood, I should for ever be ashamed of having sanctioned the
marriage.

LADY BRENDA (*almost angrily*). Ashamed of sanctioning the
marriage of Madoc with Olwen ! !   Maelgwyn, Maelgwyn, I
am disappointed in thee!   Verily thou allowest thy pride of
blood to overstep the bounds of reason !   Olwen the fair,
the adored of all thy tenants, the pride and joy of the good
monks of Rhos Fynach, the friend of the sick and poor, not
fit to wed with Madoc ! !   Madoc will not think with his
father, I rejoice to foretell.

LORD PENDARAN (*soothingly*). Brenda, my Brenda, let not
this be an occasion of quarrel between us !   Thou knowest I
would willingly sanction the fulfilment of thy dream regarding Madoc and Olwen, were I but sure that Olwen is of gentle
birth.   By my faith, it would be a joy to me to take her to
my heart as a daughter in very truth !

LADY BRENDA (*with conviction*). Maelgwyn, I tell thee that
she is of gentle blood.   Prior Cynan of Rhos Fynach, and his
brother monks, by whom she hath been educated, and to
whom Olwen is as a beloved daughter are certain of it.
Some day kind Providence will set even thy doubtful heart
at rest, and thou wilt be ashamed of ever having doubted her
good birth.

LORD PENDARAN. There !   there !   I am probably only
needlessly worrying myself, they are but young, and Olwen
would not cross my wish even though it would break her
heart, and— (*Enter servant*)

GWILYM.   My lord, there is a stranger at the gate that craveth
an audience with thee, whose appearance bespeaketh a long
journey, and who calleth himself the Lord Grey of Dorset.

LORD PENDARAN.   Conduct him hither, Gwilym.   *Exit* Gwilym.

(*with surprise*).   The Lord Grey of Dorset! the trusted
General of Henry Tudor, the King! What hath brought
him to Gwalia, and to the gate of Llys Euryn ?

(Gwilym *returns announcing* ' The Lord Grey of Dorset ').

LORD GREY (*bowing to* Lady Brenda *and the* Lord Pendaran).
I crave your pardon, my Lord Pendaran and my Lady
Brenda, for thus intruding myself on your company, but my
errand is of such a strange nature, that when you hear it,
you will, methinks, willingly forgive me.

LORD PENDARAN. My lord, say no more. I am proud of meeting with Lord Grey, whose deeds of valour on the battlefields
of France are being sung, and who was entrusted by the King
with the task of quelling the rebellion in Erin's Isle.

LORD GREY. My lord, I thank thee for thy gracious compliment.   I too am proud of making the acquaintance of the
Lord Pendaran, the faithful vassal of our King, and the son
of the brave Owain Ddu, who died on the bed, on which
most Welsh princes expire, the field of battle, and that field,
the Field of Bosworth, when Henry Tudor, the prince he
served, wrested the crown from the murderous Richard.
Proud too am I (*bowing to* Lady Brenda) of meeting the Lady
Brenda, whose goodness and beauty are the themes of the
bards of Gwalia. But a truce to compliments, for my
feverish excitement over the errand which hath brought me
here, is too great to permit my playing with fine speeches.

LORD PENDARAN. Pray, my lord, acquaint us with thine
errand, and we shall do all in our power to assist thee in any
matter in which thou requirest our help.

LORD GREY. I thank thee, my lord, for thy gracious offer.
And now, my lord and my lady, hear my tale. (*Dramatically*)
Eleven years ago I suffered a great affliction. My beloved
wife Annesta, the daughter of the Lord Argyll of Scotland,
left Dorset to visit her father, and to shew him our daughter,
then, but three months old. The mother and child with
many servants sailed from Poole, and from the day they
sailed no news of the vessel was heard of again. It is supposed that the ship was lost with all hands during the great
gale which swept over the country four or five days after
they sailed. My grief was great, so great that I have only
found relief on fields of battle, caring not whether I survived

a battle or not. Three weeks ago I was sent, as thou
knowest, my lord, to Ireland to fight the Geraldines who had
rebelled against the King ; one evening while encamped
near the sea-shore, some of the soldiers fished a weir which
happened to be near. Fish were caught, and while watching
them being cooked over the camp-fires, I overheard one of
your countrymen relate a tale concerning such a weir as that
just fished, which strangely moved me. The *year*, in which
this Welshman said the incident he related happened, first
attracted me, as it was the year in which my life was darkened through the loss of Annesta, my wife, It is his tale that
hath brought me to thy palace gate, my lord. This Welsh
soldier said that some monks when fishing their weir one
night, discovered a baby-girl in a leathern basket entangled
in the stakes of the weir. (Lady Brenda *is moved greatly and
listens attentively*). The monks, deeming the basket and
child to have been consigned to the mercy of the waves by
shipwrecked guardians, took charge of the child thus
providentially saved, and persuaded the good Lady Brenda
of Llys Euryn to rear the child. What strange spirit moved
my emotions, I know not, but the tale fascinated me, for I
connected the story with the tragedy of my life, and a wild
idea took possession of me, that the child thus strangely
rescued was my daughter. I summoned the Welshman to
my side, to repeat again the tale he had recounted, and to
give me every detail of time and place, my excitement and
strange appearance making him think me bereft of reason.
The idea that possessed me would not be shaken off, and as
soon as the rebellion was over, I hasted from Ireland to
reach Gwynedd, to make enquiries of thee, my lord, though
my idea may appear to thee, as it doth to me, a mad one.

LADY BRENDA (*very excitedly to* Lord Grey). My lord, my lord,
take heart and rejoice. Olwen, our foster-daughter must be
thy child. Truly my heart beateth gladly. (*Turning to her
husband*) Told I not thee, Maelgwyn, that kind Providence
would deal well with Olwen ?

THE LORD GREY (*feelingly*). My lady, my lady, I thank thee
for thy words. Thou dost fill my heart with gladness. Can
it be that such happiness will fall to my lot, . . . that my
daughter whom I deemed dead, should be restored again to

my arms! Kind Heaven, dash not to the ground this cup of happiness, thus strangely placed to my lips, but grant that I be allowed to drink of it! Verily, the shrine of our Lady in far Dorset, shall be richly endowed as my thank-offering, should it indeed be true that my daughter is alive!

LORD PENDARAN. My lord, calm thyself. We can only tell thee that Olwen was thus found, as the soldier related in his tale. Olwen shall be summoned to thy presence forthwith. She is even now in the banqueting hall entertaining the peasants, for to-day, St. Trillo's Day, is an high day in our parts. I shall myself go and fetch her. (*Exit* Lord Pendaran).

LADY BRENDA (*beseechingly*). My lord, should it be indeed, as in my own heart I doubt not, that Olwen be thy daughter, I crave of thee one favour, that thou wilt not altogether deprive us of her, but that thou wilt permit her to stay at times in Llys Euryn.

LORD GREY (*agitated*). Kind lady, an't please high heaven to ordain that Olwen be indeed my daughter, whom I had given up for lost, cruel would it be on my part to separate her altogether from thee, for thou hast been a mother unto her.

LADY BRENDA. My lord, I thank thee for thy words. And, my lord, thou knowest what we women are, never happy unless betrothing people to one another, and a fond dream I have ever cherished in my heart, and prayed to be fulfilled, and it is, that Olwen, when she be old enough, to wed, will look with eyes of favour on my son Madoc. (*Earnestly*) I love Olwen, and her good qualities have made me hope that she will be the help-meet of my son, and the mother of my son's children.

LORD GREY. Good Lady Brenda, surely thou art relying too much on the supposition that Olwen is *my* daughter. (*Earnestly and proudly*) Know indeed, that if she be, it will be the proudest moment of my life, when I give her in marriage to the man, that boasts such a mother as thou, and who can claim descent from the brave and godly Ednyfed Fychan. (*Stops suddenly, and assumes the attitude of listening*). I hear footsteps! . . . . . My heart beats wildly! . . . . Kind heaven, kind heaven, be gracious unto me, and grant fulfilment to the hopes of my heart.

Enter the Lord Pendaran *leading* Olwen *by the hand, and followed by* Mali, Myfanwy *and* Gwilym *whom the summoning of* Olwen *from the Festival by* Lord Pendaran *has made curious.*

LORD PENDARAN. Olwen, let me present to thee the Lord Grey of Dorset who hath travelled from afar to see thee.

LORD GREY (*advancing with agitation and murmuring softly and brokenly*). Holy Mother in heaven, I thank Thee. I thank Thee ! it *is* my daughter—*my* daughter in very truth. There are the eyes of Annesta, my beloved, looking at me,—*there* are the features of my Annesta ! (*He falls on his knees before her, kissing her hand and murmuring,* My daughter, my daughter).

OLWEN (*somewhat frightened, and clinging to* Lord Pendaran's *side*). What doth it all mean ? I do not understand.

LORD PENDARAN (*soothingly and while he speaks* Lord Grey *rises from his knees and stands looking fondly on* Olwen). Olwen beloved, be not troubled. Thou knowest the strange circumstances under which thou wast brought to Llys Euryn by good Prior Cynan, and how thou wast found by the monks in the weir. Through the merciful guiding of Heaven, the Lord Grey of Dorset hath discovered that thou must be *his* daughter, lost, as he thought, in the ship that was wrecked, during the storm which raged along this coast about the time thou camest to us, and in which ship were his wife and thou and several servants.

LORD GREY (*in convinced tones and taking hold of* Olwen's *hands*) Verily, thou art in very sooth my daughter—Annesta the good, of Argyll, my beloved wife, will live over again in thee.

OLWEN. And was my mother's name Annesta ? And was she like good Lady Brenda ?

LORD GREY. Yes, like the Lady Brenda in the goodness and kindness of her heart.

MALI (*who has been whispering to the* Lady Brenda *comes forward and addresses* Lord Grey).

An 't please your honour, though none can doubt that thou art our loved Mistress Olwen's father, yet it is well to have certain proofs. Was there no mark on thy child whereby she could never be mistaken for another's ?

LORD GREY. Ah ! now thou dost mention it, there was a mark, a curious birth-mark in the shape of a heart, behind the right ear, which now must be quite hidden by the hair.

MALI (*quite convincedly*). Of a truth Mistress Olwen *is* thy child. The mark your honour hath described hath oftentimes been the subject of talk between the Lady Brenda and me, the nurse.

LORD GREY (*in pleased tones*). And *thou* wast my child's nurse! No wonder that with a loving lady as the Lady Brenda to cherish her, and with such a kind-faced nurse to protect her, my child hath grown so bonnie and good to look at.

MALI. I thank thee, honoured sir, but praise not me. Her goodness is due to the Lady Brenda, and to the teaching of the good monks of Rhos Fynach. It will be a joy to all to know that Mistress Olwen's father hath been discovered; but alack-a-day! it will be a day of sorrow in the country round when she leaveth Llys Euryn.

OLWEN (*with surprise*). Mali, Mali, what makes thee to say that? Surely I am not to leave Llys Euryn and the Lady Brenda, and Rhos Fynach and all the folk of Glanymor. (*Turning to her father*). Sir, hast thou come to take me away? Oh, surely not! Oh! thou canst not, thy face is too noble and good to do an unkind act.

LORD GREY. My child, I shall not take thee away altogether. I want thee however, to visit mine own castle in Dorset, that I may shew thee to my people, who will be overjoyed to know of the good fortune that hath fallen to my lot. Afterwards thou shalt return to all thou lovest in beautiful Gwalia; I shall accompany thee, for mine eyes will never weary of looking on the child of my beloved Annesta.

OLWEN. I thank thee, sir, for it would break my heart to be parted from Lady Brenda, and from all the kind folk around.

LADY BRENDA (*moving forward and embracing* Olwen). And now, my lord, it would be well to take thee to Rhos Fynach, to meet good Prior Cynan and his brother monks—the good fathers who rescued thy daughter, and to whom her welfare hath always been a matter of the greatest interest.

LORD GREY. I thank thee, good lady, for reminding me of my duty. It will, in truth, be a pleasure and an honour to meet these monks of Rhos Fynach, who seem to be held in such high esteem in these parts, and to whose kindness I owe so much.

Enter Twm *of* Rhyd *hurriedly, bowing and addressing himself to the* Lord Pendaran.

TWM. An 't please your honour to forgive me for thus intruding roughly on this company, but I have just seen Father Hywel of Rhos Fynach, and he telleth me that the most reverend Prior Cynan is in great distress. Friar Roger hath been to Rhos Fynach to warn him of the suppression of all the lesser monasteries at the order of the King, and amongst those marked out for destruction is Rhos Fynach. I have hurried to tell your honour, for as I told Father Hywel, if there be any that can save Rhos Fynach, it will be the Lord Pendaran.

LORD PENDARAN (*much perturbed*). This is the first I have heard of the matter. I can now understand why the monks were not present at St. Trillo's Festival this afternoon.

OLWEN. Ah, now I too understand why they were all so troubled when I was at Rhos Fynach yesterday. The most reverend Prior told me they would not be likely to attend the festivities owing to some trouble they were in !

TWM (*beseechingly*). An 't please your honour, it would be well to go to Rhos Fynach at once, for the Duke of Somerset who carrieth out the King's command, is expected every hour, and may be there even now.

LORD PENDARAN. I shall proceed thither at once. And do thou, Brenda, my beloved, come too, and thou, Olwen, for your sympathy will be dear to the Prior and to the holy fathers. (*To* Lord Grey), wilt thou my lord, also accompany us, for thy services to the State in the field of war, may weigh with his grace, the Duke of Somerset, when we plead on behalf of Rhos Fynach, and gain his grace's favour.

LORD GREY (*readily*). It will give me pleasure to accompany thee, my lord. I know his grace of Somerset well, and perchance, I may gain his good will for this monastery. I shall do all I can, for I owe a debt of gratitude which I can never repay, to these good fathers for saving my daughter from a watery grave. (*He places his arm round* Olwen, *and all proceed to Rhos Fynach*).

END OF ACT III.

ACT IV.

SCENE.—Grounds of Rhos Fynach.

Time : Later in evening of St. Trillo's Day.

Monks *are scattered about in groups on stage, and looking much perturbed.*

PRIOR CYNAN (*in serious mood*). I have been thinking deeply over this Act of the Suppression of the lesser Monasteries, and have offered much prayer at the Shrine of St. Trillo for guidance in the matter. Rhos Fynach's revenues do not, as ye know, reach £200 a year, the sum specified in the Act as defining what constituteth a lesser Monastery, hence Rhos Fynach will be lost to Holy Church.

FATHER DEWI (*distressed*). Is there nothing that can be done ? Doth the Lord Pendaran know of our distress ? Perchance his fertile brain would conceive some way of relief !

PRIOR CYNAN. Willing as the Lord Pendaran is at all times to stretch forth a helping hand, I fear, he can avail us nothing over this matter. It will break my heart to give up Rhos Fynach, and sorrow at parting with my brethren, with whom I have spent so many years of happiness, will soon bring me to my grave.

FATHER IORWERTH. Say not so, most reverend father, thy Master whom thou hast served so faithfully, will not see thee suffer now, but will find a way of escape from this trouble.

PRIOR CYNAN. I have not lost all hope, good father Iorwerth, still it hath seemed best to prepare for the worst. I have therefore written the good Abbots of Maenan, Valle Crucis, and Ystrad Flur, asking them of their chairty to receive you, my brethren, into their abbeys. These monasteries, being great and powerful, will not be affected by this unjust act, and I know the Lord Abbots will accede to my request.

FATHER RODERIG. Most reverend father, thou art ever considerate of others, and now in this distress thou thinkest of others' welfare rather than thine own. But (*enter hurriedly* Father Caradog *who says*, Most reverend Father, the Duke of Somerset is without and seeketh an audience with thee).

PRIOR CYNAN. Let his grace be conducted hither. In this hour of trial I am as ye all, so let this King's Minister speak to all when he addresseth me (*exit* Father Caradog, *and the* Prior

The Monastery. Rhôs Fynach

turning to the monks continues). Pray, my brethren, that we be guided in this matter to say and do what is right only.

Enter the Duke of Somerset, *with his attendant soldiers).*

DUKE OF SOMERSET (*bowing to the* Prior). Most reverend father I perceive by thy countenance that I am not a welcome visitor. But be not over-hasty and class the messenger with his message. My errand seemeth a harsh and cruel one, but, by my sooth, when I enter a monastery bearing the reputation for charity and goodness that thine doth, it is with reluctance that I carry out the King's command.

PRIOR CYNAN (*graciously, but as he proceeds is moved with righteous indignation, but finishes with resigned tone).* Your grace, I thank thee for thy words. It is true that thy business is not such as to make thee a welcome visitor at any monastery, but thou dost but obey the king in this matter, and it is the evil counsel that he hath listened to that we really condemn. The justice of this Act no man, possessed of reason, can perceive, but the Church now, as often in the past, must submit to injustice and persecution.

DUKE OF SOMERSET. Reverend father, speak not so rashly and so disrespectfully of the king's decree, for such words are of kin to treason. Verily, he vieweth this Act differently to what the Church doth. But now, under your reverence's favour, I would enquire into the revenues of this monastery. On the answer dependeth its fate.

PRIOR CYNAN. Knowing what your grace's first question would be, I have made up all the returns relating to this monastery, and on this parchment wilt thou find all thou seekest to know. (*Hands the* Duke *a roll of parchment).*

DUKE (*reading*). Ah, I observe that the revenues reach but £180 a year. Hence, reverend fathers, I grieve to inform ye, that ye must leave this monastery. Henceforth its revenues will go to enrich the Crown's treasury. (*Seeing people approaching*). But who be these that approach—an my eyes deceive me not, one resembleth the Lord Grey.

Enter Lord Pendaran, Lady Brenda, Lord Grey *and* Olwen.

LORD GREY (*runs forward and kneels before the* Prior, *saying*) Most reverend father, I thank thee from my heart for the great service thou didst render me years ago, and which hath this day restored to my arms a daughter whom I thought long since dead.

PRIOR CYNAN (*with puzzled looks*). Sir, an it please thee to explain thyself, for thy action and words bewilder me.

DUKE OF SOMERSET (*aside*). Gadsooks, what is this that my Lord Grey playeth ?

PORD PENDARAN (*the Lord Grey having risen*). Reverend Prior, thou mayst indeed be bewildered, but know, that by means of the kind Providence thou hast always trusted in, it hath become known that Olwen, the child thou didst rescue years ago, is the daughter of the man that hath just saluted thee, the Lord Grey of Dorset, the trusted general of the King.

PRIOR CYNAN. Strange, passing strange, and ever merciful are the ways of Providence ! My lord, thou art to be congratulated on the daughter thou hast had restored to thee, for her price is far beyond rubies, and I thank gracious Heaven that in a small way I have been the means of saving her for thee.

LORD GREY. Most reverend father, it is I that have cause to thank Heaven, in that my child was permitted to grow up amidst such good influences as these which surround her in this part—but now the time alloweth not for me to express my gratitude to thee more worthily, for to my sorrow I hear that trouble threateneth thy monastery.

DUKE OF SOMERSET (*inclined to be indignant*). By my halidome ! am I to be left without explanation as what all this play meaneth ! My lord Grey, how thou hast suddenly appeared in Gwalia, I know not, for, methought, thou wast engaged in Ireland punishing the rebel Geraldines—but it behoveth thee to explain thy behaviour here, for know that it interfereth with the business that hath brought me to these wild parts.

LORD GREY. Pray forgive me, my lord Duke, for neglecting to pay my respects to thee, but, I know, thou wilt willingly do so when thou hast heard my story.

DUKE OF SOMERSET. Say on, my lord Grey, for I am hard pressed for time.

LORD GREY. Your grace will remember the tragedy of my life,—how, years ago, I lost through shipwreck both wife and child, and how I have mourned the loss, seeking to forget my grief by fighting in all lands for king and country. By a strange chance, I heard of a child wondrously rescued on

these shores about the time of that shipwreck, and hastening
hither to enquire, I discover that the child thus rescued, is
my daughter.

DUKE OF SOMERSET. Gadsooks, my lord, thy story soundeth
strange, and I presume that thy daughter standeth yonder
by the side of that fair lady, but what part doth this reverend
prior, whose peace I have come to disturb, play in this
history?

LORD GREY. It was his reverence and his reverend brethren
that one night discovered the child in a leathern basket that
had been washed by the sea against the stakes of a fishing
weir, which they draw every day, excepting the Sabbath.

DUKE OF SOMERSET. Marry, thy story is in truth a wondrous
one—and it grieveth me, now that I have heard it, that this
act of the King should disturb the peace of these good
brethren.

OLWEN (*rushing forward and crying beseechingly*). Oh, noble
sir, an thou hast come to harm these good monks of Rhos
Fynach, I pray thee, to spare them for the sake of the charity
and good deeds they show to all the people of these parts.

DUKE OF SOMERSET (*graciously*). Fair daughter, know that
were it in my power, it would please me much to spare this
monastery, for the sake of what these reverend fathers did
for *thee*, and for the services they thus rendered to my friend,
the Lord Grey of Dorset, but the command of the king must
be obeyed——

LORD PENDARAN (*interrupting him*). Sir, an it please thee, I
would know the exact wording of the King's Act.

DUKE OF SOMERSET. Sir, I know not whom I have the honour
of addressing——

LORD GREY (*hurriedly*). I beg thy pardon, my lady Brenda,
and thine, my lord Pendaran, and thine my lord Duke, for
not presenting you to each other. Verily, my good fortune
hath made me forget my manners. My lady Brenda, permit
me to present unto thee his grace, the Duke of Somerset,
(Lady Brenda *and* the Duke *bow to each other*). My lord
Duke, let me introduce to thee my lord Pendaran, the son of
Owain Ddu, of Llys Euryn, who died on Bosworth Field
fighting on behalf of the King's sire, Henry Tudor. The
lady Brenda, his wife, is she to whose goodness and charity
towards my daughter I am for ever beholden.

DUKE OF SOMERSET (*with a bow to* Lady Brenda). I am highly honoured in being made acquainted with thee, fair lady, for I have oft heard thy praises sung, and (*bowing to* Lord Pendaran) I am honoured in being permitted to know thee, my lord. Often hath it been told me that the field of Bosworth and the crown of England were won to Henry Tudor, by the Welsh soldiers who fought under Owain Ddu of Llys Euryn. But to return to that which hath brought me to these parts; my lord, the wording of the King's Act is as followeth— 'Every monastery whose income reacheth not the sum of £200 a year, is to be suppressed, and its revenues devoted to the King's Treasury.'

LORD PENDARAN (*turning to* Prior Cynan). Most reverend father, may it please thee to tell me what the income of Rhos Fynach amounteth to ?

PRIOR CYNAN. Barely £180 a year, my lord.

LORD PENDARAN. My lord Duke, were I to endow this monastery with land that would add to its income another £40 a year, could this monastery be thus spared from being destroyed under this Act of the King. (*Murmurs of approval from all present*).

DUKE OF SOMERSET. My lord, before carrying out the execution of my orders, thy generous offer shall be taken into consideration.

LORD GREY. Pardon me, your grace, for speaking ! But, my lord Duke, dost thou not think that the King would forgive thee thy sparing of this monastery, were it told his Majesty, that Maelgwyn Lord Pendaran, the son of Owain Ddu who died for the King's sire at Bosworth, was pleading on its behalf. I too, plead on its behalf, for though it is not I that should say it, I have given my king my best service in the field of many a battle—above all, it should be pleaded in its behalf, the high repute in which this monastery is held in this part of wild Gwalia, a fact to which all the people will bear testimony.

Enter Twm *of* Rhyd, Mali, Gwilym, Myfanwy *and all the peasants and revellers. Disturbed over their festival meal by the news concerning Rhos Fynach, they have come to plead on its behalf, having made* Twm *of* Rhyd *their spokesman.*

TWM (*earnestly, kneeling before the* Duke of Somerset). Noble

Sir, an 't please your honour to pardon the words of a humble peasant. I speak for all the people of this district. We pray thee to spare this monastery of Rhos Fynach. Ever hath it been a place whither any in need could go and obtain shelter and help. No house in this parish there is, that hath not been beholden to the monks of Rhos Fynach for a deed of kindness done to it at their hands. The fish caught in the weir are ever at the disposal of the sick and poor. Through the charity of the monks, and through their prayers, we, the dwellers in this parish are envied by the dwellers in the parishes around. Kindness and hospitality have their home in Rhos Fynach, therefore we make our humble petition to thee to spare it.

MALI (*rushing to* Twm, *and clapping him on the back*). Bravo, Twm cariad, never thought I it was in thee to speak so well.

DUKE OF SOMERSET (*pleasantly*). Gadsooks, reverend Prior, thou art indeed bless'd in the number of thy friends. By my faith, had all the priors I have visited such warm-hearted supporters, verily the King's Treasury would not be much enriched by this Act of the Suppression of Monasteries.

PRIOR CYNAN (*touched by his friends' words*). Your grace, it doth in very sooth touch me to find friends gathering around us in the hour of our trouble.

DUKE OF SOMERSET. 'Zounds, reverend prior, but thy friends gathering around thee touch me too, but in a different manner By my halidome, I am at my wits' end to know what to do ! My duty to my King biddeth me shut my ears to these thy friends that plead on thy behalf--whilst my heart urgeth me to forego my orders in *thy* case, and to bid thee and thy fellow monks stay on, and continue your good work in this wild country of thine.

LADY BRENDA (*beseechingly*). I pray thee, my lord, to list to the dictates of thy heart. Thou wilt never regret it.

DUKE OF SOMERSET. Despite thy assurance, fair lady, I have found that it is not always wise to listen to the heart.

LADY BRENDA. But, my lord, when the heart counselleth, as in this instance, a good action, surely it were wise to listen to it. They that obey the heart have ever an easy conscience, and a conscience at ease, my lord, is one of the conditions of true happiness.

DUKE OF SOMERSET. From the way thou speakest, good lady,
it is evident that thou hast never regretted listening to thy
heart's behests. It puzzleth me sorely what to do. (*As-
suming an attitude of deep thought*). Ah ! I have it ! (*Turning to* Lord Grey), My lord Grey, wilt thou be going to
Windsor soon ?

LORD GREY. I shall, your grace. I go there before returning
to my castle in Dorset.

DUKE OF SOMERSET (*eagerly*). And wilt thou be taking with
thee thy newly discovered daughter ?

LORD GREY. Yes, I desire to present her to the King, and
then to introduce her to the friends and vassals in Dorset.

DUKE OF SOMERSET (*joyfully*). Then I have it ! It would avail
but little, reverend prior, to justify my sparing of thy monastery, were I only to mention that friends spoke on thy
behalf. And (*turning to* Lord Pendaran) though, my lord,
the King might be disposed to forgive me because *thou* didst
plead on the monastery's behalf, in that thou art the son of
Owain Ddu that rendered great service to his sire at Bosworth, still it would be ill-pleasing to the King's ear to hear
how thou didst offer to supplement the monastery's income
in order to save it—but (*bowing to the* Lady Brenda, *and*
Olwen) any romantic tale concerning the gentle sex calleth
up the best feelings of the King's heart, and what story more
romantic can there be than that of Olwen of wild Gwalia,
born of the sea like the gooddess Venus ? And, an I have
her by my side to bear testimony to my tale, the King will
pardon my sparing this Monastery. Therefore, reverend
Prior, for the sake of this fair daughter, whom thou didst
rescue from the waves, I shall spare this monastery of Rhos
Fynach, and long may'st thou and thy fellow monks live to
grace it. (*Murmurs of gladness from all present*). And as
for this weir of which I have heard so much, I hope on account
of the romantic story attached to it, that the King or one of
his successors will grant a Charter, protecting it and preventing it from being destroyed at any time.
      (*All the peasants, and children huzza loudly and gather
      round the* Prior *congratulating him. While doing this they
      should place themselves in position for final tableau :—
      extreme right of stage the* Duke of Somerset, *with his soldier*

attendants behind him, next to him, Lord Grey, *then* Lord
Pendaran, *then* Lady Brenda *with her attendants behind her ;
in the centre the* Prior, *behind him the monks, in front of him*
Olwen *and* Madoc ; *extreme left of stage,* Twm of Rhyd,
Mali, *then* Gwilym *and* Myfanwy, *then young revellers,
behind, all the other peasants, etc.*).

PRIOR CYNAN. And now, good friends, with your permission
my brethren and I will proceed to the Church on the hill to
sing our praises to the kind Providence that hath blessed us,
and I invite all present to accompany us. Verily a
good action never goeth unrewarded, but (*placing
his right hand on* Olwen's *head*) never did my brethren and I
dream, that the child whom we found so strangely in our
weir, would be the means used by Providence to save the old
monastery of Rhos Fynach from being destroyed. The
benediction of Heaven rest upon thee, my child !

*All exeunt, Prior Cynan and the monks leading the way
and chanting.*

FINIS.

List of Subscribers to the 1993 Edition

Vivien Allen	Colwyn Bay	
J. Anderson	Rhos-on-Sea	
Mr J. D. Anderson	Rhos-on-Sea	
Martin Aughton	Rhos-on-Sea	
Mrs Margaret Bagnall	Colwyn Bay	
Mrs Elizabeth Barker	Colwyn Bay	
Mr A. J. Benbow	Llangernyw	3
Mr K. Blackler	Llysfaen	
Mr A. J. Bond	Rhos-on-Sea	
Frank G. Bourne	Colwyn Bay	
B. T. Bowen	Upper Colwyn Bay	2
Mrs V. Branagan	Rhos-on-Sea	
Mrs Jean Brittan	Rhos-on-Sea	
Mr A. E. B. Brown	Rhos-on-Sea	
Keith Butler	Rhos-on-Sea	
J. M. Campbell	Rhos-on-Sea	
Mrs M. J. Capel	Caergwrle	
Terry Carnall	Rhos-on-Sea	
Mrs Ruth Cavill	Rhos-on-Sea	
J. B. Chadwick	Rhos-on-Sea	
Brenda Chaplin	Rhos-on-Sea	
F. Olwen Clifford	Rhos-on-Sea	
Ven. S. Closs-Parry	Rhos-on-Sea	
Colwyn Borough Council	Colwyn Bay	
Miss V. Corbett-Roberts	Colwyn Bay	
Mrs J. B. Cude	Rhos-on-Sea	
Mr C. F. Dale	Rhos-on-Sea	
Mr D. Rees Davies	Rhos-on-Sea	
Gwynedd Owen Davies	Rhos-on-Sea	
Ivor O. Davies	Rhos-on-Sea	
Mr James Oliver Davies	Abergele	
Michael Davies	Old Colwyn	
Canon T. G. Davies	Colwyn Bay	
V. M. Davies	Colwyn Bay	
John & Maureen Douglas	Penrhyn Bay	
George David Durrant	Mochdre	
M. Eames-Hughes	Rhos-on-Sea	
Geoffrey Edwards M.B.E, LL.B.	Upper Colwyn Bay	2
J. B. Edwards	Hen Golwyn	
J. S. Edwards	Rhos-on-Sea	
Richard M. H. Ellis	Rhos-on-Sea	
David R. Evans	Rhyl	
Morton Evans	Denbigh	
Robin Evans	Talycafn	
Mrs L. Fair	Colwyn Bay	
Mrs A. F. Fairclough	Rhos-on-Sea	
Mrs Phyllis Farrell	Old Colwyn	

R. F. B. Firth	Colwyn Bay	2
A J. Ford	Rhos-on-Sea	
Miss H. A. Formby	Ysceifiog	
Councillor R. Formstone	Rhos-on-Sea	
Mrs M. E. Foulkes	Colwyn Bay	
Beti a Ben Price Francis	Llanbedr D. C.	
Mr & Mrs Eryl Francis	Llandrillo-yn-Rhos	
Raymond Gardner	Rhos-on-Sea	2
Mrs E. H. Goldsmith	Rhos-on-Sea	
J. H. Griffiths	Rhyl	
Mr J. P. Grocott	Rhos-on-Sea	
Mr H. J. Haines	Rhos-on-Sea	
M. E. Halls	Rhos-on-Sea	
Christine Hardy	Old Colwyn	
Miss Judith P. Harris	Rhos-on-Sea	
Jane Harrop	Rhos-on-Sea	
Mr & Mrs G. S. Hawley	Rhos-on-Sea	
R. John Howard	Colwyn Bay	
Dafydd Jerman Hughes	Llandrillo-yn-Rhos	
David R. Hughes	Buckley	
Elizabeth J. Hughes	Rhos-on-Sea	
John Hughes	Llangernyw	
Dr Muriel M. Hughes	Rhos-on-Sea	
Jon James	Rhydymwyn	
Mr Eric R. Jewell	Rhos-on-Sea	
Mrs J. Johnson	Old Colwyn	
Arthur P. Jones	Rhos-on-Sea	
Brian Jones	Sutton Coldfield	
Buddug Jones	Bae Colwyn	
Catherine Jones	Rhos-on-Sea	
D. C. Jones	Rhos-on-Sea	2
G. S. Jones	Old Colwyn	
Hugh Jones	Rhos-on-Sea	
Ivor Wynne Jones	Penrhyn Bay	
K. L. Jones	Rhuddlan	
Mrs M. Jones	Rhos-on-Sea	
Mrs Mary Roberts Jones	Denbigh	
Mrs Megan Morgan Jones	Llandrillo-yn-Rhos	
Neil D. Jones	Colwyn Bay	
Peter Graham Jones	Colwyn Bay	
R. Geraint Jones	Colwyn Bay	
Mr & Mrs R. H. P. Jones	Rhos-on-Sea	
Terry Kavanagh	Hawarden	
Mrs E. Lawton	Rhos-on-Sea	
Mrs Beryl Lea	Connah's Quay	
Mr G. E. Lee	Rhos-on-Sea	
G. H. Lee	Rhos-on-Sea	
A. Lees	Colwyn Bay	
Elizabeth Lewis	Rhos-on-Sea	

Mr G. C. Linch	Rhos-on-Sea
Llandrillo-yn-Rhos Parish Church	Rhos-on-Sea
A. Wyn Lloyd	Llanfair D.C.
C. S. Lloyd	Rhos-on-Sea
K. Lomas	Rhos-on-Sea
Miss Susan Maddox	Rhos-on-Sea
Mrs L. Måhlên	Gâvle, Sweden
Mr J. Malkin	Rhos-on-Sea
Mrs G. Massey	Rhos-on-Sea
Mrs G. M. Matthews	Old Colwyn
C. E. Mellish	Llanelian
Raymond Merrick	Rhos-on-Sea
J. & I. Molyneux	Abergele
M. E. Moores	Rhos-on-Sea
George Morris	Rhos-on-Sea
Beryl Moss	Rhos-on-Sea
A. T. Ollerton	Rhos-on-Sea
Miss Brenda A. Owen	Rhos-on-Sea
J. V. Owen	Colwyn Bay
S. M. Owrid	Rhos-on-Sea
Mr Gordon Palliser	Rhos-on-Sea
Mr H. Parker	Rhos-on-Sea
Mrs R. J. Parker	Colwyn Bay
Mrs Susan Parkinson	Llandudno
Mr & Mrs Glyn Peters	Rhos-on-Sea
Mr J. E. Pierce	Old Colwyn
Canon E. G. Price	Llandrillo-yn-Rhos
Councillor Peter Price	Rhos-on-Sea
Mrs W. M. Price	Colwyn Bay
C. J. Pullen	Llysfaen
Mr & Mrs Richard Raynor	Rhos-on-Sea
Ian M. Rennie	Old Colwyn
J. Rice	Glanwydden
Janet Riddler	Rhos-on-Sea
M. Robbins	Llangernyw
Mrs Annetta Roberts	Bae Colwyn
Christopher J. M. Roberts	Conwy
Mr D. W. Roberts	Ashwell, Herts.
Mr David Roberts	Old Colwyn
Mr E. Roberts	Mochdre
Eunice M. Roberts	Colwyn Bay
G. R. & M. Roberts	Llandrillo-yn-Rhos
H. G. Roberts	Old Colwyn
Heddwen Roberts	Rowen
Mrs J. B. Roberts	Rhos-on-Sea
J. L. Roberts	Rotherhithe, London
Mrs M. Roberts	Rhos-on-Sea
Peter Roberts	Rhos-on-Sea
Parch Dr John Ryan OMI	Llandrillo-yn-Rhos

Mr Reg Salmon	Rhos-on-Sea
E. M. Sandford	Rhos-on-Sea
Mrs E. M. Seddon	Penrhyn Bay
David Sherry	Rhos-on-Sea
Mr John Robert Sifleet &	
Mrs Beti Wyn Sifleet	Rhos-on-Sea
Mrs B. G. Simpson	Upper Colwyn Bay
Dr M. E. Smith	Colwyn Bay
Mrs A. Spaull	Rhos-on-Sea
Mrs E. F. Taylor	Rhos-on-Sea
Gwyneth E. Taylor	Llysfaen
Mrs Gwynne Thomas	Rhos-on-Sea
Haydn H. Thomas	Abergele
Mr A. F. Thompson	Rhos-on-Sea
Mrs S. E. Townsend	Colwyn Bay
Mrs Sue Trevelyan-Jones	Old Colwyn
D. & S. M. Tristram	Rhos-on-Sea
John F. Tristram	Rhos-on-Sea
Mrs B. M. Tyers	Rhos-on-Sea
Mr Charles Vienas &	
Mrs Barbara Joan Vienas	Rhos-on-Sea
David G. Waller	Rhos-on-Sea
Paul Weston	Pentrefoelas
Barbara White	Rhos-on-Sea
Mr A. R. Williams	Rhos-on-Sea
Miss B. D. Williams	Rhos-on-Sea
Mrs Doris Williams	Rhos-on-Sea
Mrs H. M. Williams	Abergele
Hazel Williams	Rhos-on-Sea
Hugh Williams	Old Colwyn
Revd. J. M. Williams	Rhos-on-Sea
Joseph & Irene Williams	Old Colwyn
Olive Williams	Rhos-on-Sea
Roy G. Williams	Colwyn Bay
Selwyn Williams	Old Colwyn
Mr Terence Williams	Old Colwyn
Mrs S. Winstanley	Rhos-on-Sea
Ysgol Llandrillo-yn-Rhos	
Junior School	Rhos-on-Sea
Ysgol Y Creuddyn	Bae Penrhyn